GETTING ALONG *with* HORSES

CRISSI
MCDONALD

GETTING ALONG *with* HORSES

*An Evolution
in Understanding*

Lilith House Press
Estes Park, Colorado

ISBN 978-1-7353387-2-9 (softcover)
ISBN 978-1-7353387-3-6 (E-book)
Library of Congress Control Number 2020914155

The ideas and suggestions contained in this book are not intended as a substitute for consulting with appropriate and trained professionals. All matters regarding horse training, horse care, and/or horse management should be sought out from a veterinarian and/or trained equine professionals. Neither the publisher or the author shall be liable or responsible for any loss or damage allegedly arising from any information or suggestion in this book.

Cover and interior design: Jane Dixon-Smith/jdsmith-design.com
Editor: Susan Tasaki
Cover photograph: Crissi McDonald
Author photograph: Lindsey Rashid

Lilith House Press

To the horses who continue to teach me.

Caleb, Jack, Handsome, Zephyr, Bree,
Ally, Rusty, Rocky, Tuff, and Banjo.

Thank you.

CONTENTS

PREFACE

The essays in this book come from both my monthly blog, which I've kept for the past seven years, as well as from insights that I've had since the release of my first book, *Continuing the Ride: Rebuilding Confidence from the Ground Up*.

I collected these essays out of a desire to share a different way to look at why we think horses are doing what they're doing, and possibly, to get a little closer to understanding them from their point of view. Not, *Who do I think the horse is*, but rather, *Who is the horse, as a horse?*

While as humans, we can never truly know what it is to live as a horse, I do know that introspection and decades of experience as a trainer have led me to realize how important it is that we come to our horses with a clear mind and heart.

You might find me saying the same things in different ways, or the same things in the same way. If so, it's because I often see similar patterns. For example, what are initially thought of as training issues are, 90 percent of the time, physical issues. What is seen as a bad behavior most often has its roots in a horse who's physically uncomfortable. If you can keep these patterns and what they mean at the top of your mind, you can begin—or continue—to see horses through the lens of clearer understanding.

I am certain that as long as we keep an open and flexible mind, we're able to keep learning from our horses. What they share has the potential to show us what it means to be a well-rounded horse person and a kinder human.

Crissi McDonald
Estes Park, Colorado
2020

THE BEST TOOLS

The phrase, "It's another tool for my toolbox," seems to be popular right now.

Having answers to our horse's questions is a good thing. To be with horses safely and with pleasure, there are things we must know about them. They're prey animals and running will always be their first instinct; they are faster and more sensory-oriented than we'll ever be; they have lives and priorities that have nothing to do with us.

I would also add that knowing something isn't the same as understanding it. Knowing is what I used to do before a math test: cram in information so I could pass the test. As soon as the test was done, the information vanished.

Understanding is what happened when I was in my third year of learning German. There was a point at which I wasn't translating from English to German and back again. German had its own way of being expressed that had nothing to do with English.

Thirty years of working with horses and people have also helped me grow in my understanding of both. But it wasn't always that way.

In the 1990s, when I started thinking about being a horse trainer, I was fascinated by a method heavy on round-pen work. Up to that point, my horse education had involved a lot of kicking, pulling, and making horses do things. I learned good things, too, but the overall message was that being with horses was a contest that I was supposed to win. Although I loved horses, I also was taught to use the many tools it took to train a horse.

When a cowboy demonstrated his techniques in a round pen, a technique that brought changes in horses' behavior without the use of tools, or even a longe line, I was instantly intrigued. I also realized that what I knew about horses was not much.

Over the next five years, I went to his clinics, bought all his DVDs, learned to throw a rope, read books on the method, and began working with horses my friends were having some issue with.

Nine out of ten horses responded the way the DVDs and books said they would; they learned to read my body and adjust their speed and direction. They learned to turn and face in, and we could calmly learn how to work together without a halter or lead rope.

But there was always that one horse. Every so often, no matter how much I followed the formula, the horse wasn't improving. He wasn't feeling better, and in some ways, he was getting worse. To be fair, this may have been caused by my lack of skill as much as my execution of the method. I know for sure that my focus on the method instead of the horse was a significant issue.

Even though I had more tools in my horse training toolbox, I was missing the horse. I was wandering in a forest and missing the delight of each tree. I had so many new tools and relied on them so much that I completely missed who the horse was.

It took several years of this pattern, and multiple admissions to owners that I didn't know what to do anymore, for me to start the search again. What was I missing?

I found another cowboy clinician. There wasn't a lot of dust being raised as I watched the first day of the clinic. He worked with one rider and one horse at a time. He was a kind teacher. I didn't hear, "If you do A and B, you will get C." I heard him making observations about one horse that didn't apply to the next horse. I heard him asking each rider what they wanted to do with their horse rather than going through a pre-planned lesson. I saw horses leave the arena calmer than they had been when they entered it, yet in no case had the horse moved out of a walk.

When it was my turn to ride, he watched as my Missouri Foxtrotter Jack and I gaited a few laps around the arena. He then mentioned that perhaps we could get my horse to soften a little bit.

Well, there was something I knew! After years of dressage training, I could make a horse put his head down and collect with the best of them.

Before I could begin to shorten my reins, brace my shoulders, and leverage the reins with a big bicep-popping effort, I heard, "We are going to ask your horse to soften. Right now, he's light, but not soft."

That stopped my internal chorus of "Make your horse collect" voices and stunned them into silence. I thought if I pulled on the reins and released when my horse's head went down, he was soft. Light and collected.

The rest of that session, and that clinic, I watched and asked questions about the difference between lightness and softness. In the world I had come from, the two were synonymous. This cowboy was saying they weren't.

During that four-day clinic, I started seeing how individual Jack was, and was inspired by what I could learn from him.

Working with Jack became an exploration instead of a contest. I could see how my handling of the reins caused him to defend himself, both by raising his nose and speeding up his feet. I saw how much my horse was trying to get along. I also saw how everything I knew was miniscule compared to everything he knew.

We can use accepted techniques and methods, and most of the time, our horses will respond. We can also see horses for who they are, understand that safety is their number-one priority, and do our best not to put them in a position to defend themselves.

Understanding horses, and our own horse, gives us an opportunity to experience life from a different species' point of view. How exciting is that? It means we recognize how different horses are from us, and yet how much they are the same. It means not taking anyone's word that an approach works but rather, exploring it with our horse. It means—and this is where I get excited all over again—a lifetime of learning.

Tools are handy. But so is understanding. Grabbing a tool for the sake of filling your toolbox isn't going to go quite as far as understanding (as much as any human can) what it is to be a horse.

We can forget the sticks and special halters, the crops, ropes, and martingales. With practice, mistakes, education, and guidance from our horse, we already have the best tools: the human mind and body.

LATERAL FLEXION
DISCONNECT

Polly, a chestnut-and-white paint mare, stood quietly at the hitch rail, my battered western saddle on her back and a spring breeze lifting her mane. I was chatting with her owner, finding out what was needed and how I could help them both.

Anne zipped up her jacket and flipped her long braid over her shoulder before saying, "I would like to take lessons at some point, but riding her makes me nervous right now. She doesn't stop very well."

It was 1996 and I was new to this horse-training stuff, but felt I had a solid grasp on what I did know. I asked Anne what she meant by "not stopping very well," and she said that no matter what kind of bit was in Polly's mouth, the mare would march through as though it wasn't there. Anne was only riding her in the arena at a walk; to stop Polly, she had to put the mare's face against the fence.

"Okay. I'll hop on in your arena and we'll see what's going on."

I went to my car and got a bridle with a snaffle bit. I figured if Polly didn't stop no matter what, a curb bit wasn't going to be much help.

"Besides," I said as I walked back toward Polly and Anne, "if there's something less intimidating in her mouth, she may find a way to work with me."

I unhaltered the half-asleep Polly and put the bridle on her easily.

Once mounted, I asked Polly to walk, and she did with a large, ground-eating stride. I could see why Anne would be nervous; the mare wasn't out of control, but she did like to move. Not having a way to ask her to slow down or stop could be worrisome.

Polly and I made several laps around the arena. I enjoyed the wind in my face and the feeling that if Polly and I weren't in the arena, we could cover a lot of miles. Especially if we didn't stop.

As we were neared the end closest to where Polly ate, I shortened the reins and asked Polly to stop. Since we were close to a familiar area, I wondered if that would influence her.

It didn't. Polly kept walking, now with her nose stuck out and her neck braced. I slid my left hand down the rein, brought Polly's nose around, and put her in a circle until she stopped moving. When I released the left rein, Polly took a deep breath and stood still.

"Anne, is this normally the way it goes?" I asked.

Anne smiled and said, "Well, there's usually a lot more pulling and cursing, but yes, that's how it goes."

I asked Polly to walk again, and we made another lap around the arena before I shortened the reins and asked again, and again Polly braced her neck, pushed out her nose and kept marching. I shortened my right rein and held her in a circle until she stopped.

"Well, she's pretty stiff. I've been doing something with other horses, including my own, that's working really well and I'd like to give it a try with Polly."

"Sure," Anne said. "What is it?"

"It's called lateral flexion, and it gets the horse more relaxed in their neck."

Polly and I didn't move again that day, or the next three times I came out. Our sessions now consisted of me sitting on her back and bringing her head to the left, and then to the right. Left and right. Right and left.

The trainer I'd learned this from said that you can't do too much lateral flexion, and I took that statement literally. Anne watched as over the next couple of weeks, Polly stopped fighting the pressure from the bit and swung her head to the left, and then to the right.

When I did ask Polly to go, in order to stop, all I had to do was pick up on one rein and begin to bring her nose around. Eventually I added a slight pressure from both reins, and she would stop, then swing her head to my left stirrup and then the right.

I felt like we'd hit the equine lottery. Such a simple technique, and I was proud of myself for figuring it out and proud of Polly for being so easy to work with.

Over the next several weeks in the arena, we practiced slowing down and stopping from both a walk and a trot. Polly was a star student. Every session began with bringing her nose around to my boot, left and right and left and right, before we started moving.

It was summer by the time I talked to Anne about cantering Polly.

"Sure, she canters," Anne said as she adjusted her big-brimmed straw cowboy hat. "She's got that rocking horse gait that's easy to sit. I just haven't done it in a while because, you know, the stopping thing."

"Right," I laughed. "Well, your arena is great for the work we've been doing, but I think I'd like a little larger area to canter her in. Is there somewhere close by that we can do that?"

"Yes—my neighbors have a large dirt track they ride their motorcycles on. It's big enough for a loping horse."

I bridled Polly and the three of us walked over to the dirt track. As I mounted, I looked at the path and decided which direction would be easiest on Polly. After bending her to the left and right a dozen times, we turned to our left and began walking around the dirt track.

Several times I asked her to stop, and Polly did, just as easily as she'd done when we were in the arena.

"She sure is a nice horse," I exclaimed.

Anne nodded in agreement.

Polly and I trotted and stopped, then changed direction and went through the process of walking and stopping again, and then trotting.

"All right, Miss Polly, let's see about that rocking-horse lope," I said to her as her ears flicked back and forth. We eased into a trot and I gave her a little more leg and looked down the track.

Sure enough, Anne was right; Polly's lope was gentle and easy. I relaxed into my creaking saddle and noticed that a turn to the left was coming up. I slowly shortened my left rein and got ready to lean into the turn.

Polly's nose tilted to the left. Her body kept going straight. I shortened the rein, Polly brought her nose around to my boot and loped off the track into the field. I straightened her out, put pressure on both reins and she glided from a lope to a jog to a walk and then a halt.

What had just happened? I did everything I'd been doing with other horses. I did it exactly like the book and the trainer had told me to do it. Why didn't Polly turn?

Maybe it was the direction. Maybe the afternoon sun was in her eyes and she couldn't see the path. I asked Polly to turn around and go back the way we came to see if I got the same response on the right.

Swingy walk to cushy jog to smooth lope. I relaxed in the saddle again and took a deep breath. Felt my weight drop down into the middle of the horse. Relaxed my shoulders and picked up the right rein as the turn was coming up.

Polly's nose tilted to the right. Her body kept going straight and once again, she was loping in a straight line with her nose bent to my boot.

That image sparked an aha moment for me: she was doing exactly what I'd taught her to do.

After slowing to a walk, we made our way over to Anne.

"I think I may have taught her that lateral flexion lesson a bit too well," I was chagrined by the difference in what I thought I'd taught Polly and what she had actually learned.

Anne said, "How about that lope though? I'm glad to see it's still there."

I agreed, then mentioned that I wanted to try something with Polly that would clear up how to turn and lope at the same time.

We loped to the left again and I shortened the left rein and kept a hold of the right rein, instead of lengthening it. This gave Polly a boundary and hopefully would clear up my miscommunication. Polly shook her head and then floated around the left turn. We did this twice more before turning to the right and trying it in that direction. The paint mare turned easily, even as she kept trying to bring her nose to my boot. I was struck by her kindness in the face of my mistake.

Polly was the last horse I ever did lateral flexion with. I learned from her that it can be overdone. It essentially takes away the rider's ability to steer, and it disconnects the horse's head from their body. Not literally, of course, but mentally.

I guess it surprises me that lateral flexion is still as popular as it is. From what I've seen in clinics, it causes no small amount of trouble for both the horse and the rider. Horses who are otherwise calm will swish their tails and shorten their stride even as they flop their head toward their rider's boot, which is usually giving a strong cue to go forward or move over. Neither one happens. The rider is tense, the horse is tense, and I'm convinced it's because horses and people aren't meant to live and operate in such a disconnected state.

These days, I prefer to teach horses to soften via backing up and turning. This gives them a purpose for giving to pressure. The horse is still connected to himself, both in body and mind.

If we're looking for a soft and responsive connection, it seems to me there are more effective ways of fostering that.

ASSUMPTIONS AND KNOWLEDGE

When I started training horses, I assumed I knew more than I actually did. I bought Jack, a young gelding, brought him home, and gave him a couple of weeks to settle in with my older gelding, Caleb, before riding him in the arena next to our house.

On a crisp fall evening, I caught Jack, groomed him, tacked him up, and saddled him, making sure the saddle fit. He was on his toes a little bit and moving around, but since I was a newly hatched trainer, I thought I could "train" that out of him. Once I was riding, I decided it was time to see what his canter was about. I sat up straight, made sure the reins were relaxed and kicked his sides—gently, I thought—with both heels while making a kissing noise as loudly as I could.

He left the ground like a rocket, then returned to earth running, racing around the arena and raising so much dust that I started to sneeze. This didn't help his state of mind. It became very clear very quickly that my arena was too small to contain a frightened galloping horse. I was so surprised that I forgot to do anything for a few laps. Then I came to, gathered up the reins, and applied some pressure to slow him down.

No response.

Then, I started talking to him and relaxing the reins while trying to move with him at his frantic gallop. Eventually, I noticed that, despite all the flurry, he wasn't actually going that fast.

Once we came down to a wide-eyed and hard-breathing

walk, I thought about what I'd just done. I had cued a canter as vigorously as I'd been doing with my much more relaxed and experienced gelding.

That was my first lesson in how to *not* ride one horse like I'd ridden all horses.

I didn't want to end the session on that experience, so, after a few walking rounds, I took a deep breath, relaxed, and brought my calves closer to his sides by millimeters. I was smart enough at that point not to make any extra sounds as I did this. He leaped into a canter again, but this time, he was less frantic, and I could ask him to slow down with the reins. We did this a couple of times before stopping for the day.

This memory always conjures up two things for me. First, laughter at my bravado and cluelessness, and second, the potent lesson that's stayed with me: an assumption is not the same as knowledge.

I made an assumption about Jack that had been formed by riding Caleb: horses need very big cues to know what we want. In the textbook definition of the word, I didn't know I was operating on this assumption, so instead of paying attention to the horse I had under me, I let my assumptions take control of the ride.

This is oh-so-rarely a good idea.

Looking back, if I had taken the time to be quieter—dropping my agenda for a horse I didn't know, slowing down while grooming and saddling—I would've seen how nervous he was. I would've seen that perhaps we could work on riding skills another day. I would've realized that he wasn't breathing steadily and calmly. I could've helped him settle into his new home instead of scaring the dark gray spots off him.

We usually learn to take things slowly by doing things too quickly, and the process often requires repetition to figure out exactly what's going on. The hard way sometimes has to get harder before we find out what it is we need to learn. Or, as Tom Bodett says,

"In school, you're taught a lesson and then given a test. In life, you're given a test that teaches you a lesson."

The other thing about assumptions is that it's easy to keep them alive if we don't examine them. It's also easy to mistake assumptions for knowledge, because assumptions are hidden and secret things. Horses are great at unmasking our assumptions and causing us to broaden our knowledge. Jack taught me that assumptions (in this case, all horses need big cues) are unreliable, and this realization set me on the long road to gain knowledge—both about Jack as an individual and horses as a species.

These days, when we get a new horse, we focus on finding out where the horse is comfortable and start from there. Sometimes, we can saddle up, ride, and work. Sometimes, it's haltering and grooming and leading for a day or two. Wherever we start, wherever we are in the country, and whatever horse we are working with, our goal is the same: get to know the horse and help him feel confident about us and the job at hand.

Jack taught me to drop my assumptions about what I think I know. He was also the horse who first taught me, over the course of our many years together, that a relationship built by knowledge, trust, and understanding will always go further than one built on assumptions.

THE WORDS WE USE

"My horse is such a jerk," I sputtered, the dirt flying out of my mouth as I brushed off my white shirt and listened to Caleb's staccato hoofbeats as he galloped away. He was thirteen years old, a flashy chestnut Appendix Quarter Horse with three white socks. He'd had another surprise bucking fit, and this time I'd come off. Heels-over-head, at a dressage schooling show, in the warm-up pen.

He was a skilled bucker, too, plunging his head between his knees as all four feet left the ground. This time, I sat through the first four jumps, but just as I thought he was done, he added a twist to the left and off I went, over his right shoulder. I could see why dressage saddles weren't used in rodeos.

After I recovered and remounted, we performed the best test we'd had all day. The irony wasn't lost on me when I saw the comments the judge had made about Caleb's "nice impulsion at all gaits."

Often, when I talked with friends, I told them what a jerk Caleb could be. How his bucking fits sucked, and how he was either lazy or airborne. The litany of things that I didn't like about him became longer than the list of what I appreciated.

About that time, I started going to various horsemanship clinics and listening to what the pros had to say. It was an eye-opening experience to sit for three days and not hear any badmouthing of the horses from these trainers. Up to that time, I realized that the only culture I had been exposed to was based on fighting and negativity.

I began to search for the cause of Caleb's bucking. I learned about saddle fit and equine chiropractic and bodywork, which at that time was just beginning to gain traction. I had both my horses worked on, and I also worked on how I was talking and thinking about them. I practiced keeping my mouth shut when my old circle of friends started bashing their horses. Because of Caleb, I also learned about equine acupuncture, became an herbalist for horses, and learned how to keep him sound despite his numerous physical challenges.

That was more than twenty years ago. Since that time, because of this change in perspective, because of many years of learning, and because of Caleb, I prefer to search for the good in a horse instead of focusing on what is perceived to be wrong.

Recently, I had a flashback of this time with Caleb when I heard a rider talking about her horse with words that sounded like she was beyond frustrated.

"My horse is willful, stubborn, opinionated, and lazy. He has ADD; he can't pay attention to anything, especially not to me."

In our clinics across the country, my husband and I hear these descriptors consistently, some form of name-calling, a litany of all the ways the horse isn't satisfying the owner. Most riders are eager to change their perspective, but I'm convinced their horses are waiting for the moment when their rider discovers that everything they wanted was within reach . . . that all they had to do was drop the story. One of the many amazing things about horses is that when we change, they do too.

Name-calling a horse, or anyone for that matter, may be borne of frustration or anger, but I can guarantee you that the only result will be to perpetuate an adversarial relationship. Name-calling is a lack of imagination, it shuts down our innate curiosity, and it smothers learning. Wanting to have a partnership with your horse and name-calling are at opposite ends of the spectrum. Since when does seeing your horse as an enemy to be vanquished yield a harmonious and pleasing relationship?

I get the frustration, and anxiety, and ignorance. I've felt those things too (sometimes at the same time) and will feel them again, I'm sure. If you have a horse, you've signed up for constant lessons in humility. As we go through this horsemanship journey, though, I think it's important to remember that whenever we feel like calling our horse (or ourselves, or others) names, it may be time to find another way to handle the situation.

Personally, I like curiosity. I also like the idea of pausing and breathing. Whatever your favorite strategy for dismantling frustration is, do it. You may walk away with nothing but positive things to say about your horse, and if so, your horse will thank you for it.

TOLERANCE FOR
CHALLENGES

In second grade, I remember learning two things: I needed glasses and subtraction didn't make sense. By the time I reached eighth grade, I had fought my way through the jungles of multiplication, division, fractions, and word problems, which to me, always sounded like this: If Jane has six apples and Joe has ten socks, how many cars did Bill paint?

In eighth grade, I was introduced to algebra, which gave me new ways to cry in symbols and axioms. This feeling of general panic was mitigated by the humor of my teacher, Mr. B. He was long and reedy and reminded me of Alan Alda, who played Hawkeye Pierce on my favorite television show, M*A*S*H. He was funny, too, but his humor was based on mathematical calculations. It was the first time I was exposed to math humor, and though I mostly didn't get it, I always smiled.

Algebra is when my brain ran away. While other people went on to geometry and calculus, I cried my way through fractions, word problems, and 1As minus 2Bs until panic became my default approach to any problem that had anything to do with numbers.

In high school, I had a kind teacher for geometry; he looked like Santa Claus and had the same pink-cheeked demeanor. Although this soothed my anxiety, it did nothing for my skills. If my brain ran away from algebra, it went into a coma with geometry. What made going to class easier was that a boy I had a crush on was there, too. He played bass guitar, had curly brown hair, and a motorcycle, which he took me for a ride on one afternoon after he found me crying about a geometry test I had almost failed.

If it wasn't for math, I would've been an honors student. I always ended up in remedial math classes, I had tutors, but nothing could help me once I was reduced to tears by not knowing how to find the hypotenuse of a square (or was it circle? a triangle?). I raged about how unfair it was that I had to take math when—beyond balancing a check book—I would never need it in my adult life (which turned out to be 100 percent right).

On my college entrance exams, I tested into honors English. I also tested into Math 107, a remedial course that I wouldn't get any credit for. I had to take it in order to get into the algebra course that I needed as a basic requirement for graduation.

Other than in German, English, and philosophy, I felt pretty invisible in college. Where I had (I'm embarrassed to say) felt intellectually superior in high school, I now became friends with my own mediocrity, and my own laziness.

Those two qualities are why it took me two semesters to pass remedial math. When I made it to algebra, the first round gave me such a solid beating that I spent the summer setting records at the local library for the number of books I checked out. I also set some personal records for the amount of beer I drank.

The next fall, I registered for the same course with a different teacher, only to drop out because I could see failure in my future. I reasoned that I needed a longer break, and possibly more beer and loud music, to settle down.

In round number two, I got creative. I asked my West Virginia uncle to mail me some moonshine, and I'd take two burning shots before I went to class. Turns out, some of the tests I pulled a passing grade on were the direct result of that moonshine. So were the three-hour naps that I took after finishing the test.

I ended up failing that semester, despite the moonshine and the refusal to sign up with a tutor.

I tried algebra three more times, failing once and dropping out twice. It wasn't until my final semester that I sat down once again, this time without the help of moonshine, to fight it out. Winter was warming to spring, and I wanted to be outside on the lawn, celebrating my last semester with a book and some ice cream instead of in a classroom ready to battle—once again— with math. I remember dragging my notebook and pen out of my backpack but refusing to open the thick math book that sat in front of me.

I looked up when I heard a giggly hello from the front of class, where I saw a woman who would've been more at home in the 1960s. Her dark hair fell to her waist like a straight curtain. She was wearing a cotton blouse and a flowing skirt with an orange-and-pink psychedelic pattern. And she was barefoot.

Outfits and hair didn't often catch my attention. But the bare feet made me snicker before I could stop myself. Since I had taken a seat in the back, I hoped she didn't hear me.

That semester, I had a passing grade on every test. Smiling the whole time, she coaxed what little math capacity I had out into the open. Algebra and I were now only having loud, snarky spats; the punches had stopped. While I didn't look forward to going to math class any more than I used to, I stopped panicking when letters and numbers and word problems popped up.

She taught every class without shoes. I never really exchanged more than ten words with her, but watched as she had fun with math, and in turn, encouraged us to have fun, too.

"Fun" and "math" are still not two words I will ever put together, but on the final exam, I got 100 percent on my test. She wrote the words "Good job!" in red at the top of the page. I didn't cry until I had thanked her and left class. That was the year I graduated from college, with a B in algebra.

Anytime I work with a horse who's worried or overwhelmed or even not very responsive, the first thing I feel is a strong sense of empathy, which I learned during my challenges with math. This happens with clients as well, when they're struggling to learn something new, something that maybe even contradicts what they were taught before. The anxiety of not knowing something and having to work to get better can feel daunting enough, never mind that we also need to show the horse where we're going with any given cue.

I often think horses get stressed because we do the equivalent of putting them in a class they're neither ready for nor even knew existed. We force them to do and be things that they aren't designed to do and be. Their bodies break down quicker and they become less joyful, especially around people.

The sweet hippy teacher I had removed all the pressure from a subject that had tormented my whole school life. She smiled so much and was so enthusiastic about math that it was as though I had no choice but to learn.

When I see horses who are thriving, it's usually because they're with people who understand who they are as a horse, a species, and also where their strengths are.

Although I didn't make the connection for many years, my struggles with all things math gave me a strong sense of compassion for working with horses. When they don't know the answer, or even what the question is, I know how that feels. I know the greatest gift we can give them is to approach things with as little pressure as possible and reward them as soon as they make their way to the right answer.

We go in increments. We go slowly. We're clear all the time and gentle as much as possible. This is what allows our horses to ease into learning rather than be forced into doing something by panic. This is how we create partnership.

But it's still a good idea to wear shoes with these particular students.

BARN SOUR OR DISORIENTED?

It had become a recurring pattern: I put my leg on the horse's side, and he reared up. I spun him in a circle and kicked again, and up he went. Maybe spinning the other direction would work? Kicking harder? Up he'd go, walking backward and flailing his front legs.

I had bought Jack, a Missouri Foxtrotter gelding, to retrain as a trail horse and sell, and knew that he had a habit of rearing. Although I had tried everything I could think of, and still, we were no more than fifty feet from the barn. There in the middle of the dirt road, the sun shining on Jack's gray, sweaty neck, I thought back over the past months, and of the many things I had unsuccessfully tried to get this horse to go out on the trail. Eventually, we'd get there, but the beginning was always the same. How could I sell him as a trail horse if he was so barn sour?

I decided to go back to the beginning. I rode the gelding down the driveway, returning to the barn. Before he could stop, I asked him to turn and walk up the driveway, toward the road. At the end of the driveway, we turned again toward the barn, and after getting most of the way there, we turned again and walked toward the road. This time, we went to the road, then turned and walked toward the barn. Over the course of the next hour, we alternated walking toward the barn and down the road, each time getting farther away, and farther down the trail.

By the end of our time together that day, I could ask him to walk faster away from the barn without him rearing up. Once we were at the farthest point, I dismounted, patted his now-dry neck, and led him back.

If we've been involved with horses for even a short time, we have either said or heard, "My horse is barn sour." Boiled down, it means that as long as a horse is in familiar surroundings—where he lives—he acts in a calm and agreeable way. When he leaves that place—when we take him somewhere that's not familiar—he acts in ways we don't much like. We become intimidated and from there, it's not a far leap into defensive. Much like the choices I was making in trying to force my resale horse away from the barn.

Horses look for a release from pressure and the quiet state of mind that follows. Going away from a familiar place causes an increase in pressure, and going back decreases it. In addition, returning from any kind of activity to an area where they are tied up, untacked, rested, and then turned out into a familiar place with their herd mates provides an incredibly large release. Just as there is safety in numbers for horses, there is also safety in familiar environments.

Add a poorly fitting saddle, teeth that aren't balanced (which makes the whole horse uncomfortable), feet that aren't sound, and pain anywhere in the body and the release from being ridden is even more amplified. It's no wonder they're in such a rush to get back to the barn.

When we say our horse is barn sour, it lets us off the hook and pins the blame on the horse. What we see and call "barn sour," however, has nothing to do with a horse acting out. Disorientation does, as does a horse's finely tuned sense of safety.

When you go to an unfamiliar environment, you may feel disoriented. As humans, we can rely on maps, GPS, the internet, or local people to guide us. Horses, who live by hearing, sight, smell, and the feel of the surface underneath their hooves, receive their information differently. Every time we take them away from what is familiar, they experience a rise in alertness.

We are no different; when disoriented or lost, we may feel mentally foggy, become worried, not know which way to turn, feel uneasy, or become anxious. The difference is that we can use our neocortex, the newest part of evolved brain, to formulate a plan that will calm down some of those emotions.

Horses, on the other hand, act the way they feel. There will be some sign, no matter how small, that they are experiencing a sense of worry when we take them away from their known environment. Looking at the horse as "barn sour," "spoiled," or even "spooky" closes the door on an opportunity to see beyond the behavior to what the horse may be trying to communicate.

Over time with Jack, I researched saddles and saddle fit, made sure his feet were balanced, got him chiropractic and massage treatments, and balanced his diet. I rode in or attended horsemanship seminars and clinics to improve my skills. After six months, Jack and I could ride down the trail together quietly, and the rearing had disappeared. He became my best trail horse and stayed with me for eighteen years. So much for being the kind of trainer who could resell a horse.

The experiences we shared were doorways through which I learned how to better understand him, and other horses as well. Now, I know he was trying to tell me, in the only way he could, that all he needed was time to figure out where he was, and that he was safe.

THE BIG PICTURE

Our farrier, Scott, was working on our herd, and like most times when we got together, we chatted about what was going on in our lives, mixed with talk about hoof health. After our horses had their shoes removed and their hooves trimmed, some had shoes put back on in preparation for going on the road and clinicing, and some were left barefoot since they were going out to pasture in the fall.

Scott mentioned that since people had begun domesticating horses, we've been looking for the best way to care for their feet. It began with ancient people wrapping horses' hooves in animal hide. Next, came the Roman "hippo sandal," then, around roughly 1,000 AD, cast bronze horseshoes with nail holes started showing up.

Iron (as well as steel and bronze) horseshoes have been produced and used since the early thirteenth century. Currently, the development of various types of boots, glue-on shoes, and trimming according to specific principles has expanded the hoof-protection choices.

My intent isn't to take a position in the barefoot vs. shoes debate. My point is that this casual conversation with Scott made me aware of The Big Picture. I'm unable to type the words "The Big Picture" without seeing our friend Carl use his left and right forefingers to trace a square in the air. As if he's watching his own personal movie screen. I also see his wife, Anita, smiling and rolling her eyes.

This chat made me realize that how we take care of horses' feet has a rich and varied history that spans thousands of years and multiple continents. If we could travel back in time and visit the many cultures that depended on the horse, would we see people just like us searching and experimenting and finding ways to do something that needed to be done?

This's also true of just about everything we take for granted in our daily lives, things that came into being because someone, somewhere saw a need for them. Sofas? We can thank the people of seventeenth-century France. Tablecloths? A poet named Martial (who died in 103 AD) mentioned them, and in the eighth century, Emperor Charlemagne reportedly used one made of asbestos; he threw it into the fire after a meal, and when it didn't burn, his guests were convinced of his superiority as a leader.

Or, more recently, the development of our space program. In general, it was based on our understanding of airplanes, which themselves were developed through the study of birds, but also, of wind and water currents, not to mention a whole lot of going up and quickly coming down. It's a gross oversimplification, but as I understand it, we got to space by watching nature, following the science we knew, and by making a lot of mistakes, some of which cost people their lives.

When we study something, and follow it back as far as we're able, the enormity and evolution of that something, whatever it is, is awe-inspiring.

All those eons ago, people were doing essentially the same things we are today with horses. What they did led us to where we are now, and what we're doing now will lead to what others will do in the future that extends beyond our lifetime. The idea that millions of individuals have been born, lived, invented things, and then passed on so the next generation could do the same? I feel simultaneously as though I matter and that The Big Picture will go on whether I involve myself or not.

When we study anything—horses, geology, X-rays, medicinal plants, furniture-making—we touch people we will never meet, and somehow contribute to the life of that thing. Everything in our lives, every object, every being, everything in nature, has come to exist in this moment on the backs of millions of things before it. This includes you and me, our horses, dogs and cats, tablecloths, sofas, and space travel.

What does this have to do with horses, or horsemanship? Well, it struck me with great clarity that when we study The Big Picture, we might, in the process, find a bit of ourselves. It's as though understanding something at a macro level gives us a way to comprehend it at the micro level. I've seen the way a dawning understanding of our own behavior and motivations has been extended to our horses; oftentimes, our horses are the ones who initiate that realization.

I've also seen, more times than I can count, the way a fuller perception of ourselves at both large and small levels makes things better for our horses. We ask more and demand less, giving their comfort—both physical and mental—as much priority as our own. We do things with more softness and good intent. Because we have a broader perspective, the things we do with our horses may be more understandable and approachable to them.

Reminding ourselves of The Big Picture—whatever it is— also releases us from the mindset of having to get something done with our horse yesterday. Having faith that our own and our horse's skills allows our relationship with the horse to evolve and grow. This can be felt by the horse within seconds of us making a change from a hyper focused mindset, where every detail of our time with our horse needs our attention, to the ability to work with our horse in a relaxed manner. Knowing that we don't have to get everything done right this minute relieves a lot of pressure, both from our horses, and ourselves.

For those who seek the best and most compatible equine relationships, it's very much about coaxing the inside of the horse to the outside, so that what we see in the horse is a reflection of who the horse truly is. After that, the stars are the limit.

KEEPING THE JOY
IN THE HORSE

The bay stallion leaped away from his owner as the halter slid off his roman nose. In the space of three levitating trot-strides that had him floating over the grass like a hummingbird hovers over a flower, he arched his neck and powered into a gallop before sliding so suddenly his hocks almost touched the ground. He spun, farted, flagged his tail, and cantered to the end of the five-acre pasture where his herd mates were grazing.

Solay was four years old and hadn't been touched by a trainer. Hal, his owner, a lifetime rancher, had worked with him so he could be haltered, handled by the vet and farrier, and knew how to behave around people. Otherwise, no saddle had touched his back, no trainer took credit for his gold-medal moves, and no competition claimed his talents.

As Hal and I watched Solay's acrobatics, I commented that he moved pretty well for a horse who hadn't been trained yet. Hal, familiar with my sense of humor, laughed and agreed.

Later that afternoon, Hal, Solay, and I worked on longeing. Although the rope worried him at first, by the time we took a break a short while later, he was walking and trotting at the end of it like a pro.

When I returned later that week, I watched as Hal and Solay demonstrated what they'd been working on. Hal, who had taken his homework seriously, was breathing in with Solay to a stop and directing him to a halt on an exhale.

"That looks great, Hal! So, today, I thought we would show you and Solay how to ground drive."

Ground driving isn't much different than working a horse on a longe line, except there are two lines instead of one. This is a great way to prepare the horse to learn how to turn, since each line is attached to one side of a web halter. It's also a great way for the horse to become accustomed to the feeling of a rope touching his body in different places, as well as learning how to stop softly, back up, and go forward with a cue.

Before we put the second line around Solay, we used the longe line to make sure he understood that the line around his body and above his hocks wasn't going to hurt him. Although he was suspicious of what we were doing, he remained calm, and was soon turning with minimal pressure.

We put my long cotton lines on each side of his halter, and with Hal leading him, they walked out on the circle. Hal then let go of the halter and walked with Solay as I asked him to stop and turn.

After the day's work was done, we turned him out in his pasture and again were rewarded with an equine show that made the blue sky and green grass a stage for Solay's shiny brown coat, airborne hooves, and mane that flew in the wind he created with his gallop.

That summer was spent bringing Solay along in the starting process. Hal wasn't in a hurry and neither was I. He didn't know what his plans for his elegant stallion were, but he did know that he didn't want any of Solay's spirit to suffer because of a misstep in the starting process. While I enjoyed working with both of them, what also brought me deep satisfaction was the show Solay put on at the end of our sessions. Each was different, and every time, I wanted to etch Solay's joy into my own heart.

We often forget that horses can do what they do, often in spite of us. In spite of our tension, our imbalance, our defiant grasp on the reins and our breath. A horse and rider can be poetry or a master's work of art. Horses make us grander than we are on our own two feet. Their four hooves become an expression of what moves us when no one's looking.

We often give ourselves credit for the activities horses do with us, as though we were the ones who taught them what it means to rise above the ground with such elegance. As though their balance and precision at a gallop were something we schooled. At their best, horses are who they are in spite of us. Not because of us.

All through that summer starting process with Solay and Hal, I committed to keeping Solay's joy and curiosity intact. When the day came that I, and then Hal, sat on Solay's proud back for the first time, all the credit went to the horse. Solay was calm from nose to quiet tail. He breathed with us. We breathed with him. When we turned him out in his large paddock afterward, he arced into a buck that hovered in the blue sky before galloping to join the rest of his herd.

The joy he felt, and the joy that Hal and I felt, made our world a far grander and more beautiful place than when we had started.

RESPECT: A EULOGY

"My horse has to respect me," is one of the horse world's often-used phrases, one that I hope soon has a quiet and peaceful death. I've invited it for walks to discuss other points of view. Helped get its affairs in order. But this phrase, I discovered, was born without ears. It needs a funeral with no gathering of friends and family afterward.

While I've been a grateful witness to an evolution in horsemanship (for example, I hear much more often about horses being "started" rather than "broken"), our need for our horses to respect us seems to have its feet glued to the floor of our collective unconscious.

Even without hearing it from well-meaning horse people, the internet is littered with videos and articles, chat rooms and equipment to "make your horse respect you." Here are some of the quotes I found when I googled "horses" and "respect."

"Your horse's respect for you isn't automatic; you have to earn it. The best way to do this is by moving his feet forward, backward, left and right. The more you can move his feet, the more control you have."

"A horse who understands that you, as the herd leader, own the space in which he lives, will respect your asserted authority."

"Without respect, you have nothing; no relationship, no trust, and ultimately, no communication."

But here's the thing. Respect is a human concept. To force another species to observe it without regard for their own needs, social structure, or intelligence is ill-informed at best and abusive at worst.

The human brain, or more specifically, its newest component, the neocortex, is what allows us to form and use abstract concepts like "the day after tomorrow," "robbing a bank is wrong," and "my horse needs to respect me." Respect is part of a complex human-to-human social interaction, and one of the ways we get along with each other.

It may be a fairly large deductive leap, but I'm going to make it: because the horse's neocortex isn't well developed, it's difficult for me to believe they have the ability to form abstract concepts. I also don't feel it's a coincidence that what some call a horse being "respectful" looks a lot like a horse who's afraid. Though it might not be the intention of the handler, what we teach, and what horses learn, can be vastly different things.

If we've absolutely fallen in love with the word "respect," let's respect that:

- Horses are thinking, feeling, living beings who feel both mental and physical pain.

- Horses will hide pain and discomfort as long as they can.

- Horses form powerful friendships and rely on the herd as primary to their safety.

- Horses are hardwired to survive and get along. They will cooperate, even at the risk of their own well-being.

- Horses have rich inner lives and ways of perceiving the world that are wildly different from ours.

- Horses don't owe us anything. As horse owners and riders, we are not entitled to their power or skill or courage just because we house and feed them.

I've seen horses who understand boundaries once they know where they are. Horses who rely on consistency. Horses who have a job and are happy to perform it with us. Horses who need direction. Horses who are disoriented. Horses who rely on the relationship they have with a person. Confused horses. But I've never seen a respectful horse, or a disrespectful one, for that matter.

It makes as much sense to say that whales can climb mountains.

"My horse needs to respect me" opens the door for us to commit grave errors. It sets up a mentality of competition, of winners and losers, and, at its worst, legitimizes fighting with the horse.

Between a human and a horse, it is far less about the horse giving us what we need than it is about us figuring out how to encourage that great big heart to come out of hiding.

If there's any respecting to be done, my vote is that we respect ourselves and our horses and become as educated and skilled as we can. We can then work with them in ways that allow them to trust themselves in our hands, and on their backs.

FIRM RESOLVE, GENTLE APPROACH

Grace, a little paint mare, stood trembling at the end of the longest lead rope I could find. The July morning had dawned hot and we were both sweating in the middle of her paddock, though the cause of her agitation was probably due more to the bottle of fly spray in my hand.

Her owner, Tammy, said that every summer, Grace would tear off her fly sheets, ruin a half-dozen fly masks, and be covered in flies from her sunburned nose to her constantly swishing tail. Fly spray was out of the question and trying to wipe it on wasn't any easier. After two summers of watching Grace suffer, and out of options, Tammy wanted to see if we could help her little paint horse through the issue.

Thinking about Grace's response to fly spray, we decided to change a couple of things. First, we filled an old spray bottle with water, then we let her run loose in a round pen. I stood in the middle of the pen and began spraying water to the side of me and toward the ground. Without a halter and lead rope to contain her, the mare took off at a run. Initially, there wasn't much change; she kept running, I kept spraying. Any time she put an ear or an eye toward me or thought about slowing down, I would stop spraying. As she started to understand that facing the sound caused it to stop, her frantic run slowed to a canter, and then a trot.

In less than twenty minutes, Grace was able to stand still without a halter as I sprayed her with water, starting at her hooves and moving up to her legs. Her neck and body took a few minutes more, but she was standing quietly not long after. We had been working together for about an hour when I told Tammy we both needed some water and a break.

Afterwards, Tammy and I went back into the pen, haltered Grace, and reviewed what we had done. The mare needed to move again, so we let her. After a few minutes, she quieted down and let us cover her with spray.

We took another break, then brought out the fly spray. We poured a little into the bottle so that the smell changed and, starting at her hooves, worked our way up her legs and onto her body. Though Grace wasn't likely to put this on her list of Things That Are Great, she stood still. We repeated the process a few more times in her paddock, then untied at the hitch rail where she was usually groomed. Although she felt the need to move around, the level of fear that she initially felt was almost non-existent, and after moving, she would then stand quietly.

We took another break, this time so we could bring out the real fly spray and see what Grace thought about that. Standing in her paddock wearing a halter and lead rope, she was quiet as the fly spray went on. I patted her still sweaty neck before slipping the halter off and walking out of her pen.

The reason I share this story is that, so often, we think what we do with horses has to be done right dang now. It doesn't. Though there are some things that do indeed have an immediacy to them, that doesn't mean that we have to do them quickly or with a hard hand.

Granted, Grace was being tormented by flies and needed some relief, but even then, we took our time, gave her breaks, and watched her closely so we could time the release (stopping the spraying sound) to the moment she was even a tiny bit curious about it.

I have often heard that horses don't wear watches. They also don't have deadlines. But what they do have is a very clear sense of pressure. When we force them to stand still out of a misguided sense of having to get things done right this second, the result is a perfect storm of miscommunication.

Though our resolve should be firm, our approach doesn't always have to be. Erring on the side of gentleness and slowing things down often make things exponentially easier. By remaining aware, calm, and doing our best to work with the horse, we can often get things done in a manner that leaves the horse feeling better about the situation than when we started. As far as I'm concerned, that's on my list of Things That Are Really Great.

THE SPIRAL OF LEARNING

If horsemanship is a spiral of learning, the outermost ring would be figuring out how to safely handle them, learning the physical aids of riding such as how to use our hands and legs, and how to efficiently balance on a horse's back.

Another turn of the spiral, and we learn to make cues more subtle. We apply them with better balance, timing, and feel.

Once horse people are several revolutions into this spiral, however, many of them sometimes get stuck, or plateau. One day, our horse becomes less responsive, and we give bigger cues. We feel stagnant. Or we have a horse who stops responding to any technique we know.

Whatever the reason, the result is the same: at some point in our time with horses, we realize that what we know and what we're doing aren't improving the way we spend time with them.

The good news is that there's a doorway within every horse. If we're quiet and still, that doorway becomes the portal through which we can reach the next turn of the spiral.

What is this doorway?

It is the opportunity to connect at a level that underpins the essence of who horses are, and who we are as well. It is a tether to communicating at a level older than human language. Horses are masters of this language, as is most of nature. We are, too, and it only takes a little practice to rediscover it.

This language, for me, closely resembles the way we feel when we listen to our favorite music as opposed to when we need to, say, figure out a work problem.

One way to begin strengthening this sense is by using the thought and/or intention of "we."

When a rider gives a physical cue and the horse responds, that's an example of a fairly superficial communication. It's what is sometimes referred to as "conditioned response." We give a physical cue, and through systematic training, the horse learns to execute the desired action.

The good stuff, the grit and substance of working with horses, however, spirals much further down, to exploring the movement beginning inside of us. We are walking, we are trotting, coupled with feeling the rhythm of the gait. Our intention is to build a bridge from the inside of us to the inside of the horse.

Now, the sequence would be to visualize and feel "We are trotting" before we offer the physical cue.

This change of intention is essentially like using a turn signal to let other drivers know where you're going. Since riding (like driving) can be a non-verbal activity, we have developed signals to let the horse (other drivers) around us know what we intend to do.

Our change of intention does two things. One, it lets the horse know, before we apply a physical marker, what we would like to do. Two, and more importantly, it creates a sense of togetherness. It's no longer us doing something to the horse (squeeze with the leg, lift the rein, and so forth); rather, we are now doing the same thing at the same time.

If we ride using only physical cues--which is not a bad thing, by the way--horses will operate that way. If we ride seeking to use more subtle aids such as changes of intentions/thoughts or the way we breathe, they will go that way, too. The art of horsemanship lies not only in subtlety, but also within the hearts and minds of both participants.

The art of horsemanship is a combination of the human and equine spirals of learning. There is potential for the horse's spiral and our own to mesh, or synchronize. Oddly enough, or perhaps not, this appears elsewhere in nature. I like to picture it as a double helix strand of DNA. It's a useful image for what happens when we combine our talents with those of our horse.

Our horse Rusty has given me the opportunity to learn the power of combined talents, along with the power of potential.

Soon after he was dropped off at our barn, we could tell there was more going on than standard fatigue. Over the next several months, he was aloof. He couldn't be caught, and, when he was, submitted to our care or to being ridden with an air of defensive resignation that was painful to witness. Once the halter was on, his eye went dull.

After we had traveled with him for a year and had helped him feel better physically by balancing his feet, body, and teeth, we turned him out on a 35-acre pasture for the winter. We were hopeful that a human-free, six-month rest would recharge him.

It turned out that he had eight months off before Mark and I loaded him up and hauled him to a series of clinics in California. He was less worried, and catching him was easier, but he still didn't interact with us much.

Because he was having trouble keeping weight on, I started hanging a hay net in front of him while he was standing tied throughout the day. I found a supplemental feed he really liked and started mixing in herbs that would help his stomach. I noticed he was pretty thin-skinned and sensitive to grooming, so I only used rubber curry combs and soft brushes on him. At first, his workday was about a half-hour of riding and a whole lot of eating. As the weeks went by, our saddle time and his eating time began to balance out. By our last clinic in California, his eyes were bright and his ears were forward. His muzzle, once jammed up and wrinkled, had softened and relaxed.

We were getting to know one another. A horse who I at first sought to help because it seemed like he needed it was quickly becoming a trusted partner who ended up being to help me, too.

Up to this point, we had been working on him being able to carry himself with his head down at a relaxed walk and trot. I had also been asking him to respond to the internal cues I was offering instead of having to use a lot of leg or rein cues. He was opening up, and our time together was not only easy, but peaceful. I had a sense that Rusty was almost ready to show me who he was. Almost.

On the last day of the clinic, Rusty was feeling settled at the halt, walk, and trot. Once we were in the trot, I thought about cantering with him, and offered a change of rhythm in myself first by going from the two-beat of a trot to the three-beat of the canter. He tensed a little at this and rushed through his trot. I breathed more deeply and switched from a sitting trot to a relaxed posting trot. We did this for another lap, and I asked for the three-beat again, this time using a bigger exhale, and a tiny bit of leg against his side. He rolled into an easy canter, with the kind of energy that makes a lap around an arena a short trip. He never got faster, but the canter got more powerful. It was as though he had rediscovered how to use his body. It even felt like he was enjoying it.

We cantered for another couple of laps before we changed to the four-beat of a walk. When we stopped, although he was breathing hard, he was quiet and the reins were loose.

I dismounted, patted him on the neck, then sat down so we could both digest what had just happened. When I was seated, Rusty walked over slowly and stood with his head over my lap, eyes closed and breathing deeply.

As I sat with the sun warming my back, I realized that I had needed help, too. Like good friends do, Rusty had offered his help. He had shown me what it's like to break through an internal barrier, and what life feels like once we're unburdened by the drag of past hardships.

We walk, we trot, we canter. We can focus on the doing-ness (walk, trot, canter), or we can focus on the we-ness. That double helix of horse and human is just waiting to be accessed.

Our horses will do just about anything we ask—their nature allows this. But a horse doing something with just his body is a far cry from a horse doing something from his heart.

The same could be said of us.

LIVING IN THE CENTER

As we stood at the gate to the horses' paddock on a sunny afternoon, my nephew Quinn said, "Aunt Crissi, I want to pet every horse in the pen!"

"Let's do that," I said. "Before we go in, though, let's breathe and feel our belly. Horses really like it when we're breathing and centered." He took a fast breath and slapped his hand on his stomach.

Quinn is an energetic ten-year-old given to bursts of jumping, spontaneous singing, and loud talking. I love his exuberance but wanted to give him another way to focus when we went in with the horses. Most of our horses like and understand children, but a couple of them look sideways these little beings and their quick movements.

I opened the gate and Quinn darted in. I reminded him about breathing and feeling his belly. I added, "It's also called your center, and it's the place where you and the horses can meet."

He waited for me as I walked in, still chatting quietly about breathing and feeling our centers.

The horses had just been fed and were stuffing hay into their mouths as quickly as they could chew. They stood around the feeders, heads down, eyes half closed in gastronomic bliss. When we got part-way into the paddock, all of them lifted their heads, left their hay, and walked over to us.

A rush of horses always thrills me, but this was an even bigger thrill. It was as though we had said "Hello friends," and they were answering with a resounding "Hello" back. It felt like that moment in the movie *Arrival* (or, if I really want to date myself, *Close Encounters of the Third Kind*), when the characters realized they were actually communicating with an alien species.

I spoke to him about reaching for their shoulders or necks instead of their faces (despite the fact we were surrounded by six horse faces) and brought him closer to me to keep him from being jostled.

Quinn and the herd exchanged their mutual admiration, then, one by one, the horses returned to eating.

When we walked out, he gave an arm-flailing little hop and said, "That was so cool!"

As I walked over to my niece who was grooming Ally, I asked her to focus on the same things. She's a quiet and kind girl who is very gentle with the horses. They, in turn, are quiet with her too.

Keyvnn has been riding since she started visiting us in Colorado. When she was small, I let her know that when we ride a horse, we always groom before and after. Now that she's big enough to push a wheelbarrow, the list of tasks has expanded to cleaning pen and stalls as well as grooming. Just as I was at her age, she is happy to participate in all things horse, and I love seeing her growing confidence.

This year, we had Key focus on her belly (center) and breathing not only during riding but when she was grooming Ally as well. This gave Key time to acclimate to Ally, and it let Ally feel confident in Key's presence.

Sharing our horses with my niece and nephew was a great way for me to explore how to phrase and teach concepts I normally talk about with adult riders. It was also a chance for me to see just how powerful remaining in our center can be, and how it radiates out.

If we pay attention, life gives us just the right lessons at just the right time. Most of my life, I haven't paid attention, so these days I'm working on reversing that trend. Whenever I'm feeling threatened by world events, this refresher on the power of our center is just what I need. It's been on my mind that, with all the bad news available to us every day, it's sometimes difficult to figure out how to remain centered.

Remaining in our center is anything but passive. It takes self-control, lots of breathing, and a fair helping of awareness, especially when we feel drowned by details and out of control. I'd been distracted from being in my center, but Key and Quinn's visit reminded me of the power of living there, and how we can return any time we choose. They gave me just the right amount of help exactly when I needed it. That is part of living a centered existence as well: the capacity to ask for and accept help.

Although it seems that sometimes our lives are everywhere but the center, if we take a breath and change our focus, just for a moment, we can touch the place where we feel most balanced. We can balance exuberance with calm, and gentleness with breath. The beauty of horses is that they will meet us there, every time.

FIDDLIN' AROUND

After twenty-eight years away from playing music, I decided to start practicing the violin again, working on some drills that involved moving the bow across the strings at different speeds. I've always practiced these techniques slowly and increased the speed as it felt more comfortable. Every day for two months, I practiced. My shoulders locked; my wrists stiffened; my breathing stopped; and that sneaky, mean, low-down, nasty voice in my head said, "This is too difficult!" and "You sound atrocious!"

But then, when I started on the bowing drills—yet again—something clicked. Suddenly, I was bowing like top-notch fiddle player, producing a machine-gun barrage of unstoppable notes.

I laughed, then put my violin away.

It occurs to me that we could apply this same commitment to doing things mindfully with horses.

Horses are Grand Prix–level dressage stars pretty much from the time they're born. Side passing? No problem. Roll backs? Child's play! Capriole (a movement where the horse leaps into the air and kicks out his hind legs)? Piece of cake. Flying lead changes? Easy peasy.

It's only when we get involved that things become a little more difficult. Side passes, roll backs, flying lead changes—even just backing up—can all feel heavy and difficult and require a ton of effort.

But when we're able to make a couple of small adjustments, things get easier. The first adjustment is breaking the process into smaller chunks for both the human and the horse's benefit. The second adjustment is creating a pattern of sorts, something we can do with and away from our horse over and over until our bodies sync up and the movement happens almost of its own accord. Then the pattern disappears, and it's you and your horse doing something together.

An instructor/horse trainer who can guide you through these patterns and what it takes to learn them can be useful with this, but the rest is up to you.

You get to choose how much to practice, how often to practice, and if that practice is of importance to you. This's why you'll often hear us say that in order to get your horse going more softly, you need to find ways to go more softly yourself. Can you drive softly (i.e., breathing deeply and steadily, letting go of your competitive mindset, loosening your white knuckles on the steering wheel)? Can you groom and touch your horse with focus and an intent to be soft?

When I talk about patterns, I mean the things we do to create the muscle memory that allows us to skillfully participate in a task with our horse. A great horsemanship skill is breathing. How many times a day do we remember to take a deep breath, in and out? How many times a day do we catch ourselves using more muscle, and muscle tension, to perform any number of tasks—making the bed, taking a shower, mucking the stall, sitting at our computer. Many of us carry tension in our shoulders because we've become numb to it. We've practiced shoulder tension so much that relaxing it no longer occurs to us.

So, how often during our day can we close our eyes and drop our shoulders? Relax our hips and spine? Shake our arms and let the tension drain away? How we do anything during our day-to-day routine is often how we do everything else in our life. By the time we get to our horses, is it a wonder that they feel spooky and tense? Oftentimes we've been jumpy all day long, too.

The work that my husband and I do with horses asks that we also pay attention to ourselves. To get better at being with horses, we believe that we need to get better in our lives in general. Finding softness with horses is very much about finding softness with who we are.

There's no need to feel ashamed of a habitual way of going through life. Rather, it gives us an opportunity to look at how we do things, and to take the tension out of our bodies while we do them. We can remove the tension from our minds and hearts for just a moment, until that particular pattern becomes a part of us.

On those difficult days when you feel like the fumbling and mistakes will never end, can you put that sneaky, low-down, mean little voice in the backseat?

I believe you can.

I believe we are all capable of striving toward the places that make our hearts sing. Horses know these songs. We can too.

RELEASE AND RELIEF

We seem to learn and go through life much like a pendulum; we swing all the way to one side and then all the way to the other before realizing that the middle is where balance and skill lie. Once we find that sweet spot in the middle, that space goes from a thick, black line drawn with a Sharpie to fine one scribed with a mechanical pencil.

In between those wild swings of the pendulum of learning are the stages of competence. A theory developed by Martin M. Broadwell in 1969 and initially called "the four stages of competence," it became known as "the four phases for learning new skills" in the late 1970s, after Noel Burch from Gordon Training International took it further.

1. We don't know that we don't know. (Unconscious Incompetence)

2. We know that we don't know. (Conscious Incompetence)

3. We know but we have to think about it. (Conscious Competence)

4. We know and can complete a task without thinking about it. (Unconscious Competence)

As children, we grow up watching an adult drive a car. We don't think anything about it. We get in, the car goes, we get out somewhere. This is stage one: We don't know what we don't know.

At some point, we learn to drive. Wait a minute! This's a lot harder than it looked! We are running into stage two: We now know that we don't know.

Depending on our skills, we'll reach stage three pretty quickly if we're allowed to practice. We can now drive, but we really have to think about it. How to stop the car. How to get through a four-way stop without crashing into someone. How to make a left turn. How to back up without hitting anything (not that I did this. Multiple times. Not at all).

By the time most of us are in our twenties, driving is a non-issue. We get in, we drive where we need to go, we park, get out, no problem. We know how to drive and we don't have to think about it. How many of us go back and forth to work, or to the barn, and barely remember the trip?

In the town where Mark and I live, a roundabout was installed at a busy intersection. This meant that for four months, the way we usually drove to the barn was closed. To take care of our horses, we had to take a different route. I won't mention the number of times we both got in the car, the car went, and we encountered—surprise!— a "Road Closed" sign. We both laughed at how much thought it took for us to not go the way we'd been going for years, and to plan a new route. As tourist season started, even the route we'd worked out suddenly became too busy, so we had to find yet another way. I don't think either of us ever reached the stage of Unconscious Competence, but we got close.

When we begin learning about horses, we start at stage one. This is true for all the skills we need to learn to safely be around horses, but none so much as learning how and when to release.

Many of us know that when we're teaching a horse a new skill, we must provide a release of pressure to show the horse he got it right. I'd been doing this to some degree from the time I began riding as a child. Shortly after I started training horses, I encountered a way to be more conscious about it at clinic given by a well-known horseman. I'd arrived at stage two: I knew I didn't know.

When I started systematically applying the release, it worked really well. It wasn't too long before I came to the realization that if a little release was good, more was better. This included completely letting go of my reins if the horse I was working with did whatever it was I was asking. I would stop all work immediately if they hit on the right answer. You name it, I released it. The pendulum had swung to the opposite extreme of where I began when I learned to ride; instead of releasing infrequently, I now released for everything.

For a couple of decades, I continued to practice and refine my skill of releasing. I got pretty good at staying at stage three, Conscious Competence. I was always searching for that middle space where the release was not too far one way or another, but right in the middle. I learned that horses are sensitive beyond our wildest imagining, that big releases were, most of the time, not necessary, and indeed could send an unintended message. When I learned that, back I went to stage two.

But it wasn't until we spent some time with Dr. Steve Peters—a neuropsychologist, horseman, and co-author of *Evidence Based Horsemanship*—that I learned that, for optimal learning, the horse must experience both release and relief.

If I were a horse, I would've pricked my ears forward and thrown my mane in the wind.

As Dr. Peters explained it, the more time a horse is given to process a new skill, the more time there is for the nervous system as a whole to move into a state of relief. The chemicals that were present during the pressure of learning or doing something new dissipate and the feel-good chemicals, specifically dopamine, are released. Simply put, the greater the relief (the more dopamine), the greater the learning.

How do we achieve this hallowed state? By giving our horses time. It's not a big deal if they don't know things. If they seem to have to think about it awhile. If it takes some time for them to perform a skill so that it feels easy and automatic. They are making their way through those same four stages.

Despite our perception that we don't have time and our busy lives are too full, we could stop and consider that it is entirely within our power as riders and horse owners to give horses the time and understanding they need to feel confident with us. A little understanding goes a long way toward feeling peaceful together. A little more time is something we can all find for our horses.

SOMETIMES, DOING NOTHING IS DOING SOMETHING

"Can you come out and help me get my horse into the trailer?"

Carol was selling her horse, Bertie, and needed to get him to his new owner. Her distraught voice on the phone told me all I needed to know about how the previous trailering sessions had gone. Carol was a lifelong horse owner and competitive trail rider, so she had experience on her side, but she clearly found this to be unsettling. It wasn't static breaking up her voice, it was worry.

Although Bertie had loaded and unloaded well previously, he was now refusing to get into the trailer. He would be the new owner's first horse, and Carol didn't want to add the burden of reteaching him to load.

When I arrived, I saw a large bay gelding standing tied to a hitch rail across the dirt driveway from a two-horse, straight-load trailer hooked to a pickup. The trailer was at least twenty years old but had been well taken care of, its fresh coat of white paint and new hardware catching the afternoon sun. Glancing at the horse and back at the trailer as I walked up, my initial thought was that the big horse had every right to ask if he was going to fit in that small space.

I'd barely asked Carol to tell what she'd already done before she was talking about her history with Bertie.

It turned out that he had arrived in this trailer, and she

had even hauled him to a couple of trail rides in it three years prior. But recently, when she brought him up to the trailer, he stopped. The more she forced him, eventually cracking behind him with a longe whip, the further she was from loading him. Turns out, Bertie was talented at running backward. During the most recent attempt, following the advice of another trainer, she attached a longe line to the trailer and ran it around Bertie's hindquarters to try and leverage him in. Bertie had responded by rearing.

When I asked Carol if she would show me, with Bertie, what that looked like, she gave me a skeptical glance before untying the gelding and walking him toward the trailer. Bertie shook his head, cow-kicked with a hind leg before planting his feet, and attempted to rear. Carol turned and walked him away, then tried again. This time, farther away, Bertie not only stopped, but turned his large head away from Carol and tried to quickly move both of them away from the source of such contention.

Telling Carol that she could stop, I took Bertie's lead rope and stood quietly by him, waiting for him to take some deep breaths and also to show him that I wasn't here to fight or force him. When he stopped twitching his tail and put his head down, I patted him on the shoulder and waited a few moments longer.

When Carol was leading Bertie, I noticed that there was a zone in which he felt comfortable, and a zone in which he didn't. My first question to him was, could we stay in that safe zone together and take some breaths?

As he calmed further, my next question took the form of leading him two steps forward, close to the edge of his comfort zone, and stopping again, waiting for him to breathe.

In this way, we got five steps closer to the trailer before turning around, walking away, and stopping to breathe, farther from the trailer than where he and Carol had ended up earlier.

As I turned and began walking toward the trailer, I felt a change in the tension on lead rope—a pressure that hadn't been there before. Instead of stopping, I changed direction and went to my left, turning Bertie in a circle before continuing in the general direction of the trailer. When we got as far as we were before, I stopped, patted his neck, and waited for his breathing to slow down.

We repeated this pattern—taking Bertie away while he was calm and not going so close that he felt he had to defend himself—for an hour. At the end of that time, we were within six feet of the trailer, and while he wasn't as calm as he was when farther away, he wasn't rearing or trying to drag me away.

I motioned Carol over and explained what I had been looking for, and how well Bertie had done.

"I can't believe he's been so calm," she said, scratching his jaw. "I mean, he's usually like this, so the whole trailer-loading thing really took me by surprise."

"Well," I smiled, "I imagine it took him by surprise, too."

As the three of us walked away, I noticed that the sun was on its way back behind the mountains. Time didn't concern me much; I had blocked out the day for Carol and Bertie and wasn't in any rush.

We chatted for another ten minutes, then I told her I'd like to try again and see what Bertie said about the trailer.

This time, the lead rope never changed in my hands. I heard the drumbeat of his hooves behind me and looked down to see the dust swirling around our feet.

Within four feet of the little white trailer, I stopped. So did Bertie. I took one step closer, fed the lead line out so I could walk closer, and touched the divider and the stall doors, which Carol had thoughtfully tied open so they wouldn't swing.

That's when I felt the lead rope tighten and heard Bertie give a hard exhale. I glanced behind me, but stayed where I was, relaxed my left leg and continued my inspection of the trailer. I felt the lead rope tighten to the left, then the right, and out of corner of my eye, saw Bertie pacing at the end of the rope. I stood still.

Within thirty seconds, the rope went slack and the dust

started to settle on Bertie's now-damp coat. I stood. I waited. We breathed.

The lead rope was now slack in my right hand, so I brought my left hand up and touched the divider, brushed some dust off of it and glanced at Bertie over my shoulder. He wasn't moving anymore, and he wasn't breathing much, but his head was lower, and he was giving me a chance to show him what my intentions were. After a moment, we turned away from the trailer and walked away.

The second time we approached, we were both close enough that I could step in and look at the feed mangers, look at the divider, and look at the floor mats. I didn't stamp around or make a lot of noise, just held the lead rope and put my gaze everywhere but Bertie. The big bay gelding didn't move. I took this chance to have a seat at the edge of the trailer and check the sun's path in the sky.

Bertie put his head down and sighed. He licked and chewed and cocked a hind leg. Maybe I wasn't the only one who needed a rest.

Once I stood, up came Bertie's head and, for extra good measure, he backed up a step. I turned around, stepped into the trailer, and started my inspection again. Leaned on the divider. Breathed in the scents of hay, manure, and the pine trees surrounding the property.

Bertie took a big inhale and blew out through his nose, the water droplets landing on the dusty trailer floor. At this point, I left the trailer and walked him far away from it.

I noticed that at some point, Carol had gotten a chair and was watching us work from the shade of a pine tree. I waved and asked if she had any questions.

"No, you really haven't done anything yet for me to ask about."

I smiled at Bertie and thought that he probably felt we had done a whole lot.

Back we went to the trailer, and now I started rattling the

doors, moving the divider, and trying to make the noises that most trailers make.

Out of the side of my eye, I saw Bertie pacing again: left, right, left, right. Stop. Lower his head. Breathe. Lick and chew.

Through all of his movement, I kept moving things and making noise, watching to make sure that what we were doing wasn't too much for him. I stepped up into the trailer and, almost absentmindedly, gave the rope a little pressure, just to see what Bertie's answer would be.

He stepped forward. And forward again. I was glad the emergency door was open, because it occurred to me that Bertie might think I wanted him in there with me. I stood still and watched as he smelled the door, the divider, the floor, then once again cocked a hind leg and looked at me with eyes that were relaxed and bright.

"Well, Bertie," I said. "Aren't we moving right along with this whole trailer thing?"

When I walked away with Bertie behind me, I made my way over to Carol and asked if the divider was easily removed.

"I think part of what's going on is your big gelding here doesn't feel comfortable in a space the size of a single stall. If we can make the whole trailer more like a box stall, he may find a way to feel better about getting in."

"Yeah, sure," Carol said. "It's super-easy to do, even with one person."

I led Bertie farther away while she got the trailer sorted out. I noticed how he was breathing and looking at the trailer as several loud thumps and a bang announced that the divider was free.

Bertie and I walked up to the trailer and I walked in again, feeling the lead rope slack in my hand.

I heard Bertie's front feet thump onto the matted floor. I thought to myself, *Isn't that an amazing sound?* I didn't turn and face him, but kept an eye on him over my shoulder.

He sniffed the wall, the window screen, the opposite wall,

and then, for the first time, pointed his nose toward the front, sniffing the fresh hay Carol had put there.

I backed up toward the manger (and the emergency door), and Bertie took two more steps and stopped. I waited. We breathed. I asked him to back out.

As we walked away, I mentioned to Carol that loading a horse into a trailer has several parts, and if any of those parts cause stress, the horse can change his mind about how safe he is in a metal box.

The first part is the approach. This is where Bertie and Carol had had some misunderstanding. Once we explained to Bertie that we could approach the metal box in a calm state of mind, he could feel safe about putting his front feet in.

The second part is the horse being able to load himself, or feel confident and calm about following someone in. I normally stay outside the trailer when horses are loading; an agitated 1,200 pound flight animal (in Bertie's case, probably closer to 1,400 pounds) in a small enclosed area is not a ride I particularly want to take. But in this case, Bertie was calm and I had an easy out through the large emergency door at my back.

The third part of a horse's trailer-loading skill set is remaining calm while the doors are closed. This can be the most worrisome part for a lot of horses, and there are many ways to help them feel better about it.

"Carol," I said, taking off my hat and wiping the sweat from my forehead, "Bertie's done a lot today, and I know you said you need to get him to his new owner right away, but I sure would like to do this right so he's not an ounce worried when he leaves. Can we meet again tomorrow morning?"

Smiling, Carol said yes, and I handed Bertie back to her.

The next morning, I decided that in the future, I'd schedule summertime trailer-loading lessons before nine a.m. The air was brisk, and a small breeze washed through the pines as I got out of my car and went to find Carol and Bertie. I looked at the hitch rail, then glanced at the trailer and saw Carol sitting on the floor, petting Bertie's lowered head.

"Well, look at you both!" I exclaimed as I walked up.

"Yes, I was curious and wondered if he would get this close with me. We haven't been doing very well when it comes to trailer loading, and I wanted to make up for it." I could see Carol had done a lot of thinking overnight.

"Excellent! It doesn't look like Bertie has any hard feelings."

Carol handed the lead rope to me and the three of us stood quietly before I turned with Bertie and walked a short distance away.

I could feel a difference in the big bay horse this morning. In addition to his hooves solidly striking the ground with sonorous thumps, the lead rope was so loose that I had to take up the slack. I looked over my right shoulder and saw Bertie, head down and swinging, following me with his eyes half-closed.

I walked straight into the trailer and turned just in time to see Bertie follow me in; one, two, three, four thumps later and I slid out the emergency-exit door and stood on the trailer's running board as Bertie nosed the hay, then took a mouthful.

We stayed that way for a while; there's almost nothing I like better than listening to a calm horse eat. Then I put a little backward pressure on the lead rope and asked Bertie to back up. After taking another mouthful of hay, he did. I stepped back into the trailer, followed him out, and walked him toward the hitch rail.

Carol followed us, stammering in her excitement that it had "happened so quickly!"

I grinned and said, "You remember the three parts to trailer loading we talked about? It looks like Mr. Bertie here was confused about the first part, the approach. Once we calmed that down and gave him a bit more space, he felt pretty good about getting in."

"Can I give it a try?" Carol asked. Relief and happiness were written all over her face as I handed her the lead rope.

"Sure! Just take it slowly and remember to step outside onto the running board. I'll be here in case you need me."

Carol led Bertie, both of them breathing. Bertie's head dropped and his feet thumped four times, raising dust that the wind carried away. Carol went in the trailer, Bertie stepped in behind her. Standing outside of the emergency door, Carol put her feet on the running board as Bertie once again began to eat.

After a few moments, I showed Carol the cue I used to have him back up. She asked. Bertie ate. She asked again, Bertie took an obliging step backward, then resumed eating. Carol turned and smiled down at me.

"I guess he doesn't want to get out now."

"Well, let's give him another moment and ask again. This time, instead of releasing when he takes one step, keep a light pressure on the lead rope and see what he does."

Carol asked Bertie to back up and keep backing, and he lumbered his big bay body out of the white trailer. It doesn't seem nearly as small as it did the day before.

"There are two more parts before we're sure that he's okay in there. Let's close the emergency door but keep the hay manger windows open. I'd like to see if he'll load without being led in."

I took the lead rope from Carol as she shut the emergency door and opened the manger windows.

"Well, that's how he used to load, when I got him." She said as she released the latch and opened the window, shoving hay back inside.

"That's good news. Let's see what Bertie thinks of it today." I turned, took Bertie a short distance away, and led him to the trailer, this time staying on his right side.

He paused before the trailer, his head going up and his tail swishing. I stood. Breathed. Kept his nose pointed toward the front of the trailer. Bertie backed up two steps, shook his thick dark mane and scattered dust into the morning air before coming forward again and sniffing the floor.

I saw Carol rocking back and forth, as if her movement could help him in.

"Hey, Carol?" I brought Carol's attention to me. "Can you take a big, deep breath?"

She laughed and nodded, then stood still. So did Bertie.

I waited a few moments, keeping Bertie's head pointed in the direction I wanted him to go before leading him away and turning to try again.

The lead rope was relaxed in my hand but it didn't have the swing of the day before. *That's okay*, I thought. *Small steps.*

At the trailer, I again stood on Bertie's right, turned toward him, and, with a kiss sound, asked him to think about going forward. Bertie hesitated, then one, two, he had his front feet in and was stretching his nose toward the hay. Carol let out an exhale. I might've, too.

I asked Bertie to back out, led him away with the lead rope swinging, and repeated the same process.

One, two, three, four thumps later, he was eating hay. Carol pantomimed applause and I smiled in return. I then picked up the lead rope, said "back," and stood aside as Bertie stepped out of the trailer. Again, we waited there for a few moments until his head lowered and he was breathing more calmly before leading him away once more.

We didn't get very far away from the trailer before I turned again and asked Carol to untie the doors so I could start swinging them open and shut. With Bertie standing behind me, I opened and closed the doors, latched them, unlatched them, and did the whole thing again. When I looked back at him, his ears were forward, but his hind leg was cocked, so I carried on being a loud human. He watched, then lowered his head again.

"Carol, can you close the left door and hold the right door for me? Let's still keep those windows open, though."

Carol latched the door and held the right door open. I walked with Bertie toward the trailer, and, four thumps in as many seconds later, he was munching hay. I took the door from Carol and started swinging it back and forth. I knocked on it and closed it and opened it and kept an eye on Bertie, who only had eyes for his hay.

"Huh," I muttered.

"What?" Said Carol.

"Looks like he's fine in there. It really was the approach that scared him the most. The rest of this, he's like an old pro."

"So, do we close him in and deliver him today?" Carol asked.

"Let's get him out and go through the whole process as though we're going to do just that. Then we can decide."

Carol opened the door. I put a little pressure on the lead rope, said "back," to Bertie, and stepped aside as he once again slowly put each hoof back on the ground.

We walked away. We turned around and this time, I swung the lead rope over Bertie's broad bay back before he stepped into the trailer. I closed the door and latched it while Carol watched Bertie through the open manger window.

"He's eating!" she said.

I went around front and gathered the lead rope from his back and tied him to a hook that was above the window. Stepping down from the trailer, I turned to Carol and said "My vote would be for you and Bertie to do this a couple more times before you haul him away. Do you want to do that?"

"Sure! No problem," Carol said.

Ten minutes later, Bertie was eating in the trailer and Carol was shutting the manger windows. As she wrote me a check, she grinned and said, "I can't believe I'm paying you for doing nothing."

"Sometimes," I said, "doing nothing is doing something."

WHERE'S YOUR LINE?

I have a little puzzle for you:

How would you make this line shorter?

_____

Erase it? Cut it in half? Scribble on it?

Instead of defacing the original line, you could simply draw a longer line underneath it.

_____

_____

We often use this thought experiment when teaching our horsemanship courses because it illuminates a pretty common way of thinking. Sometimes we get so caught up in how someone else is doing something wrong or bad that we forget to put time and energy into finding ways to increase the length of our own line.

If you look at the lines as representing skill sets, you can see that shortening someone else's "line" is what happens when we choose to run people down. I'm not talking about giving up your opinions or beliefs. Rather, I think that if we consistently turn our focus to lengthening our own line, we will not only gain more skill, but feel happier as well. Because there's nothing like a little comparison to make you feel anything but happy.

Shortening other people's line doesn't only pop up in horsemanship circles. It seems these days are especially fraught with commotion. It's incredibly easy to get pulled off the focus of our life. There have been many times recently when I have forgotten my personal ideals—or ignored them with something that felt very close to relief—in order to indulge in negativity. It's not a coincidence that the increased time I spent paying attention to the news decreased my drive to pay attention to my own internal workings.

Because developing our own skill set is challenging, right? It's much easier to forget basic manners and blast someone for all the ways they're wrong. Then celebrate all the ways we're right. Erase their line, and ours doesn't have to grow a bit, does it? I like the way my husband Mark says it: "There's a big difference between wanting your horse to be better, or wanting to be better for your horse."

Our ability to increase our skill is in direct relationship to our ability to keep our focus on what is truly important for us. A focus on being better for our horses is miles away from making our horses better. The first is in our control. The second? Well, it's only the horse's good nature that lets us believe the illusion that the latter is also within our control.

When, in a state of dissatisfaction, we turn our attention outside of ourselves, it seems we cannot help but try to erase, cut in half, or scribble out other people's lines. I am convinced that this gets translated to our horses as an increase in pressure for them to just get it *right* already.

Conversely, there is also the voice that tells us our line will *never* be as long as another person's, so what's the point in even trying? (I fall into this trap when I practice the fiddle.) So what if you and your horse can't *piaffe* or *passage* like an Olympic medalist? So what if you can't spin at Mach 1 like the horses at

The Congress? Besides the cost to the horse to get to that level of skill, there is the plain truth that we are who we are, with the skills that we have, and the choices we make either bolster those skills or let them get rusty.

I have seen, in myself and others, that once we focus on being better for our horses (or better in our life, for that matter), a natural slowing down happens. We become more thoughtful and more likely to experience the joy of the moment. We pay less attention to things that aren't important and more attention to the depth and weight of our own lives, which is really all we've got anyway.

We can accept where we are and grow it, or we can fight. Either way, our horses are on the receiving end of our decisions. It seems if we want quieter and more peaceful horses, it would be a good idea to make choices that support that same state of mind for ourselves.

SMALL SHIFTS

When we're learning about horses, most of the time we're taught to look for big things. A buck here, a pinned ear there, and we're caught in the illusion that we can understand at least most of what a horse is trying to say to us.

Those signals do indeed give us information. But I've found that the really rich stuff lies in a change in the breath, a closing of an eye, a soft drop of a whiskered lip. A long, deep sigh.

What about the puzzle of a cocked hind leg and wrinkles around the eyes and mouth, or ears held out sideways—is that relaxation or not feeling sure? Most horse puzzles can be sorted out by looking at context. A horse standing with her hind leg cocked, drowsing while tied to a hitch rail is different than a horse with a hind leg cocked, head up, and eyes wide. I'd see the latter as a horse who wanted to rest but was unsure of her surroundings. In that case, we'd do our best to help our horse feel better about what was going on, which would allow that cocked hind leg to signal true relaxation.

Small shifts are where the conversations with horses get richer. We begin to read them not only with our eyes, but also with our ears, our nose, and that bass-drum beat in our guts. Hang around horses long enough, practice listening deeply enough, and bit by bit, their world opens up in starburst color.

This isn't to say that we always know what's going on with them—sometimes, we barely know what's going on with ourselves or those closest to us. The journey of knowing both our own horse and also horses with a capital H is a lifetime-long endeavor, in all the ways that word implies.

In my own journey as an equine bodyworker, which began in 2014 when we met Jim Masterson, I was fascinated by how a light touch could elicit a huge release from a horse. With this method, I watch for the eye blink that indicates the horse feels something in the spot on which I lightly rest my hand. Then I wait, not increasing or decreasing the pressure, or moving my hand. This is the difficult part for many of us: waiting to see what happens. Jim jokes that his method came from being naturally lazy, but I'd like to think that it also arose from the fascination with how small we can be with horses and how big their releases can be: from yawning, licking, and chewing to lying down for a nap. Aside from my husband Mark, Jim's the only other equine professional I've heard say, "When in doubt, go softer."

Most of modern horsemanship is rife with the opposite teaching: when in doubt, get bigger. Phases of pressure. Make the right thing easy and the wrong thing difficult. The trouble is, the right thing is already difficult, as is the wrong thing. Besides that, how is the horse to know what's "right" or "wrong"? She only knows that she feels safe or she doesn't. She can trust her world or she can't.

We are either part of a horse's small shifts toward a calm state of mind or we aren't. The only thing increasing pressure does is decrease the horse's sense of safety. I know now that a little pressure is needed for learning, but when the scale tips from a little to a lot, we get ourselves in trouble. Or damage a horse's trust in us and what we're asking her to do.

We need more softness and more gentleness in our lives, and we need it in this present moment. Every day, we have an opportunity to slow down a little bit, to notice the moment when we walk to meet our horse and she sees us. To see how she licks her lips, lowers her head, and greets us without a big fuss. After all, in a herd environment, big fusses are what get herd members injured, or eaten.

What small shifts do we need to embody to step into their world? What can we do to shift our consciousness, even just a little bit, so we are a space of quiet in an otherwise noisy context? What adaptations can we make so we can see their world through their eyes, if only for brief moments?

These are the questions that guide my own horsemanship and why I regularly practice meditation. Why I seek out information on what we're learning about horses. Why I enjoy reading about and watching others who, in their own ways, are doing their best to communicate with horses outside the domination paradigm.

Horsemanship is riddled with myths about how to make horses do things; if you listen long enough to two horse people talking, you're likely to hear a saying someone else passed along to that person, because they, in turn, were told by someone else they hired to teach them, who was, in turn, told that thing by someone they learned from. Add in the internet and chat rooms and social media, and now we aren't even learning from knowledgeable people we trust. We've become three times removed from the source of all this fervor, which is our horse. In short, we're entering the land of mythology.

Myth: A story with fictitious characters, magical happenings, and extraordinary events; an unproven or false collective belief that is used to justify a belief, a value, our sense of being right, and so forth.

What's happening outside us gets filtered through our experiences, beliefs, opinions, and wishes until it fits our personal model. Until it looks like something with which we are comfortable. Until it is either one step or fifty away from the truth of the situation. We know that if you ask ten people to observe an event, you will get ten different versions of that event. Similarly, ask ten horse trainers how to teach a horse a certain skill, and you'll get ten different answers.

We each have a network of knowledge about horses based not only on our experiences with them, but also, what others have told us is true and correct. Add to this that our perceptions may be skewed, and I think it's a perfect opportunity to reconsider what might be happening when the words we use about our horse show them in not a very positive light.

Between the Masterson Method® of bodywork and our dedication to looking for softness, whether in life or in horses, I've become acclimated to small, soft shifts so that when a big startle happens with a horse, a ripple runs through my body like electricity. I wonder if this is what fear feels like to horses—a current of energy that makes it impossible to stand still. If that's the case, I'm becoming even more aware of why what we do as humans is so loud to horses, and what saints they are for doing their best to get along with us.

Although a true revolution in horsemanship may be in the future, I believe the numbers of people who have the horse's best interest in mind are increasing. Improvements in the ways we think and talk and interact with our horses, and for the benefit of all horses, are on the rise. If you need evidence, take a look at book titles from the last fifty years. What began as a trickle is now a flood. What began as a small shift in our perception of horses is now a big movement toward improving their lives. Even things we see as small can surprise us with how vast they turn out to be.

RIDING INTO RELAXATION

We sometimes forget that horses already know how to perform any action we need them to do. They are movement PhDs—they can fly (briefly) without wings, run fast, jump high, and move in ways that lose us in the awe of their artistry.

What we do as riders is attach a cue to a particular movement. There's nothing fancy about training horses; as long as you understand when to release and when to cue, working with a horse isn't rocket science.

Creating a space where the horse willingly does those moves for you, and is so confident that the movement is relaxed? *That* is the art of horsemanship. You can't buy it, cheat it, manipulate it, or fake it. I will gladly spend the rest of my life pursuing this art.

If you have a horse long enough, he will associate you with either relaxation or with tension. With feeling safe, or not.

This's why when I hear riders complaining that their horses are "stubborn," I feel drawn to ask how we can reframe what they're feeling. What if we, as riders, aren't breathing, or have our shoulders up so high they look like chunky earrings? What if we have a horse who's reading every—dang—signal—our bodies and emotions are broadcasting and haven't a clue which ones to respond to? The good news is that all of this is within our power to change.

I get being at the end of your metaphorical rope when the same behavior shows up again and again and you don't know what to do about it. When all you want to do is make your horse's actions match the picture in your head.

When there's a gap between what we'd like and what our horse is doing, the first place we can look is at ourselves: What are we doing—or not doing—that the horse interprets in a way that makes her tense? The second place we look is to our horse's physical needs: Does she need bodywork? Nutritional support? Teeth and feet balanced? Tack that doesn't interfere with how she needs to move? In our clinics, we more often see horses who have physical issues rather than training issues. My best guess is that 10 percent of the horses we see have true training issues. That means that 90 percent have something else going on.

After those questions are answered and the physical problems are resolved, we're then working with a horse who's able to do what we need her to, whether it's cutting a cow from a herd or performing piaffe or walking down the trail. The next question is, how do we ride our horse into the relaxation of the movement rather than in tension, which limits how well she can perform?

As I was walking with the dogs one afternoon, leaning forward a bit to look at the different shapes of their paw prints in the dirt, it occurred to me that we spend a great deal of time hunched over. We hunch over computers, hunch in a chair or our bed to watch television, definitely curl up around our smart phones or tablets, sit hunched and tense behind the wheel of our car. We hunch over the sink to do dishes and when we sit down to eat a meal. Some of us even walk slouched over.

Becoming aware of how we hold ourselves is what will help us start to not only ride our horses into the relaxation of movement, but also, begin that relaxation in our own minds and bodies. The great thing about horses is that because we need to be balanced in order to stay on, hunching while in the saddle is not a good idea. Keeping our eyes on the ground and staying in a slouch while we are grooming or doing groundwork is also dicey. Horses require us to look up, to straighten up, and to use our bodies in non-habitual ways. They are so much healthier for us than screens.

The practice of riding in relaxed physical balance is a good way to develop the skill of riding in emotional balance. To me, this has the quality of a meditation practice, minus the cost of a three-day silent retreat. Each day, I find a quiet space and sit for five minutes, not only watching my breath go in and out but also marveling at how much like breeding bunnies my thoughts are. These racing, bouncy brain waves are everywhere, reproducing at an alarming rate, hopping from here to there and outwitting my breath at every turn. Needless to say, they're a barrier to the much-coveted empty mind.

Riding is the same. If we drive to the barn shaking our fist and cursing at other drivers, then expect to have a quiet and centered ride, good luck. If we walk out to our horse's pen fuming about an argument we had and expect our horse to greet us eagerly, that particular wish may not happen. Riding our horses into relaxation is all about us relaxing first.

But it's a gradual process. Like meditation, we need to build our being-in-the-moment-with-our-horse muscles. If we dive in too soon, we will frustrate ourselves. If we don't practice at all and let those bunnies in the saddle too, frustration is a sure bet.

Instead, we shoot for a present and happy walk. We take a breath, we feel the warmth of our horse's soft neck, see the particular shape and tilt of his ears. And then we take another breath and practice staying present and open in the trot.

We need to convince our chatterbox brain that it really is okay to take a break and listen.

Sometimes we help our horses, sometimes they help us. I don't mean to say that everything in your world needs to be rainbows and lollipops. Life happens all the time. It's more about finding ways that are meaningful to help us set aside our concerns and worries while we're with our horses, so we can give them the full attention they need, and deserve.

We need and deserve our own full attention, too. We can ride ourselves into relaxation, just by the choices we make each day.

REMOVING
MENTAL HOBBLES

In response to requests from several of our online classroom members, we posted a photo on our Facebook page of one of our horses standing hobbled. We also made a three-part video series that carefully explained how to teach a horse to be okay with hobbles.

The lesson that followed minutes after posting what I thought was an innocuous photo were filled with insight. And humility.

We thought this photo was just a photo. However, for others, it was an example of cruelty and abuse. It was a source of disappointment that we would advocate their use. How could we?!

Mark and I have both worked on ranches where hobbling is just another job a ranch horse does, like standing tied or moving cattle. Neither of us had used this as a way to punish or scare horses, and I personally have never seen a hobbled horse hurt himself. But it quickly became apparent that, for those who didn't share that background, it was an example of horse abuse. The other interesting thing was that the angry comments we received were about the photo, not the video series.

A few folks felt that by hobbling a horse, we were taking away his ability to flee. That it may induce learned helplessness. That we were setting them up for both mental and physical injury. To be fair, all these things can certainly happen if a horse isn't properly prepared for the experience. Hobbling isn't something you do with a horse who has limited life experience and training.

It's not a way to force him to stand still. And it's certainly not a substitute for teaching him how to stand while tied. But, when done appropriately, hobbling is an extension of their education.

However, what interests me isn't the hobbling debate. It's the insights into human behavior. Who we are in life has a direct impact on how we are with horses. Those two days of seeing unbridled anger at our post provoked me to think about a few things.

At some point, each of us runs up against our own beliefs and prejudices. If we aren't careful, that translates into our horse work as a certain rigidity: my horse *has* to do the thing, right *now*, in this *exact* way.

If we aren't careful, our view of our lives, and of the world, can get pretty narrow. And small. Small isn't where life thrives. Small is where we dig ourselves in because we feel threatened. Life—and horses—live big and open and out there.

Some of the most aggressive people I've ever encountered profess to be kind to animals. They spend hours learning about horses or dogs or cats or whatever pet they may have. They put a tremendous amount of effort into understanding and caring for their pet. When it comes to relating to other people, though, they make very little effort to understand or get along.

These are the people who sometimes, when they find a social-media post that's at odds with what they believe, attack first and don't ask questions later. I can only guess at their motivation; it may be to force someone else to change, or at the very least, to shame the other person, or make that person feel like a horrible human.

I get it. Despite being deeply introverted, I've spent my adult life working with the public, and I often struggle with human interactions. In the past, I've often said that I get along better with animals than people. If I had a horse for every time someone else has said that to me, it would be a vast herd roaming the plains.

I realized when I started teaching that getting along with and being kind to animals is easy. Getting along and being kind to people is where the challenge lies. Kindness, or any positive quality we wish to have, is robust and full-bodied and inclusive. One might say unhobbled.

How can we call ourselves tolerant if we only apply that tolerance to certain people or certain breeds or certain riding techniques and/or disciplines? How can we be patient if we only practice patience when it suits us?

After reading the comments in the hobbling post, I saw that the people who were against hobbling honestly felt they were correct. I also saw that we needed to be more thoughtful about what we place on social media, keeping in mind the broadness of our audience and its individual life and horse experiences.

Though I strongly believe we are all more alike than different, the one trait I don't care to share is close-mindedness. It isn't helpful in horsemanship, or in life. Having a closed mind feels awfully similar to living in Smallville. When I run into closed places in my own mind, I'm aware of how much easier it is to leave them that way. Sometimes, I go around those doors, sometimes I open them up, with a lot of WD-40 and trepidation. I'm still trying to figure out the difference between closed spaces and boundaries. It's getting clearer—better lighting helps—but it's still no treat.

In order to be the kind of teacher and human I want to be, I have many skills to learn. Some of the skills I work on daily are things my introverted self would really rather avoid. Some days, I want to (and do) sit on our couch with my cat and a good book and let the world go on its way.

Right now, though, I'm grateful for the commenters' angry responses because they brought me to these personally valuable realizations. An experience like this, though fleeting, helps me get closer to who I want to be. Like working with horses, I'm not striving to be perfect—just a little better than I was before.

JUST BEING HUMAN

At a daylong retreat, I had an opportunity to chat with one of the speakers. I approached him, introduced myself, and let him know how much I appreciated his work. We got to talking about the words people use to describe his work, and him. Both his easy laughter and chagrin at some of the terms felt familiar to me. We shared thoughts about how such labels, while on one level helpful, could also be limiting. Toward the end of our conversation, I remarked, "We have to use labels, because it certainly isn't enough to just be a human being!"

Later, I rolled that around in my head for a while—the idea that we enforce on ourselves (and, perhaps by proxy, others who come into contact with us) the idea is that "being human" is not enough. We have to be this person with this talent doing this incredible thing while striving to stay ahead of some imaginary curve by which we measure ourselves.

Often, we extend this to our horses: they are not just horses, they are breeds; disciplines; trophy-, money-, and award-winners; therapists; best friends; teachers. The way I see it, labels are neither bad nor good. But sometimes, they're like driving on ice: one quick turn of the wheel and we're in a ditch.

Of course it's fun to do things with horses. Of course we like challenges and improving our skills with horses. Of course they can be our friends, teachers, and confidants. All of that and more! At the end of the day, though, they are horses, just as we are humans. Personally, I've found that letting go of labels (as much as we can) brings a certain quality to our interactions with others and with our horses. By its very nature, striving to see things as they are depressurizes most situations. It can mean the difference between fighting with a "stubborn" or "resistant" or "lazy" horse and clearly communicating what we're after to a horse who is otherwise unclear about our request. Once we see things as they are rather than as we wish they were, we can interact with them in a productive way.

I've seen Thoroughbreds who didn't like to run. Warmbloods who were happier out on the trail than in an arena. Quarter horses who loved to jump, Arabians who excelled at working cattle. I've seen gaited horses perform fancy dressage moves and child-sized ponies who had more of a say in herd dynamics than the bigger horses.

My point is, despite the labels we give our horses, they are so much more than those labels. Sometimes we recognize this, and sometimes it takes a horse (or several, in my case) to jar us out of our tight-fisted, white-knuckled grip on a label.

Many years ago, while helping out at one of Mark's clinics, I said to him (with no small amount of frustration) that the horse I had brought with me was fifteen years old and "should know how to be bridled" by now. Mark paused, then observed, "Maybe if you treat him like he doesn't know, instead of treating him like he's fifteen, it might go better." That was the beginning of my grip starting to loosen, and sure enough, once I calmed down and helped my horse understand, we stopped fighting and things got easy.

Lesson: Confusion doesn't know—or care—how old you are.

Another lesson: I didn't have to keep beating myself up about not recognizing what my horse was trying to say. I changed how I was asking, my horse changed how he responded, and we went on to the next thing.

I guess, in a way, it's like traveling back to when I was twelve. Grooming a horse or riding a horse—any horse—felt the same to me. Joyful. As I got older, I did a small amount of showing and a large amount of comparing myself to others. When I began training, I did my share of pressuring a horse to be something different than what he was. My share of agonizing over and struggling with how to get my horse to do something I felt was *very important*. Perhaps it's a by-product of getting older and working so closely with them, but these days, I feel as though I'm still that pig-tailed girl who's giddy just to be hanging around a horse.

Horses are many things to many people, and by no means have I seen it all when it comes to horse/human interactions. But I've seen enough to say with confidence that when we're able to see and treat our horses as they are, things usually go pretty well.

HORSE, INTERRUPTED

As I walked to the arena to help Dave with his sorrel gelding, Whip, I could see that the day's session would begin at speed. Wide-eyed and snorting, Whip was flinging his head in every direction, and Dave was doing his best to hang on to Whip's halter.

"Let's let Whip move around a bit. Do you have a longer lead rope, or a longe line?" I asked.

Incredulous, Dave turned to look at me, dodging to avoid Whip's head as he did so. He gave the halter another tug and bent down to pick up his hat from the dirt before answering me.

"I don't know if that's such a good idea right now," he said between short, huffing breaths. "I think I'd rather just help him get settled down. He doesn't do real good in any new place, but sometimes if I can make him stand still, I can get on and we can go to work."

"How's that worked out in the past?" I asked as I watched Whip lift Dave off his feet by throwing his head so high that I wasn't sure it was going to stay attached to his body.

"Well, it's hit or miss," Dave admitted, once his feet were back on the ground. He then added, "Mostly miss, if I'm being honest."

"Tell you what, let's let him move a bit and if that doesn't seem to be working, we can try something else. Deal?"

Dave released the halter, handed the lead rope to me with a small smile of relief, and said, "Deal."

When you ask people if they consider themselves good listeners, most will answer that they are, usually after having either finished your question for you or answered before you were done talking.

We don't need to look far to witness this kind of behavior; tune into any radio or television show and you'll hear raised voices competing to be heard. Interrupting has become a form of social dialogue, and whoever talks loudest and fastest often gets the most attention. We seem to interpret this behavior as acceptable because when we go out into the world, we feel it's okay to not let the person we're chatting with finish—or even have—a say of their own.

Increasingly, I've noticed that when I meet someone for the first time, they will almost always blurt out a question in a kind of machine-gun barrage of words. I used to reply the same way. But because I've had this nagging suspicion that neither I nor the person who sought an answer felt good about the interaction, I've begun to change my response. Instead of answering the question, I'll reply with "Hello," or "Good morning." Ask how they're doing, and what their name is. When they ask the question again, it's often slower, not to mention more coherent.

I find myself slipping into the habit of interrupting as much as anyone else; not a day goes by that I don't catch myself. Perhaps it's our current Culture of Me, or social media, or the chaotic events that so often surround us. Whatever the reason, engaging in a polite, coherent conversation seems to be far less sexy than having our say no matter what. If we aren't careful, we'll find ourselves applying "having our say" to interactions with our horses.

Whether they're trying to let us know about a physical problem or poorly fitting tack, or that they don't understand what we're asking them to do, horses communicate all the time. If we don't know how to guide them to what we want (sometimes *we* don't know what we want), or if we aren't listening because we've labelled them "spooky," "stubborn," or "cranky," the behavior sometimes escalates. Bottom line, labels relieve us of the responsibility to find out what's driving their behavior.

After we got a longer rope and let Whip take off just under the speed of sound, two things happened: he was able to start breathing, which in turn helped him calm down, and we let him have a beginning, a middle, and an end to what he was communicating.

In other words, instead of interrupting him, which sounds something like this …

Whip: I'm—
Us: Stand still.
Whip: But if I could just—
Us: Behave!
Whip: I—
Us: You'll feel better if you would Just. Calm. Down!
Whip: I NEED TO—

We did this:

Whip: I'm worried! I need to move!
Us: Okay. We're going to stay in a circle in this part of the arena and you can move as much as you want.

Whip grew calmer and quieter throughout the lesson, which confirmed that we were headed in a good direction. Over the next two days, he and Dave made great progress as we practiced listening to what Whip had to say, and ways to answer that helped both of them feel better.

We are often so busy talking, and we think what we have to

say is so important, that we forget the other person also feels the same way. Though communicating better with our fellow humans can certainly be difficult, I am convinced that applying it to our horses will yield fuller, richer, and deeper communication with our equine friends.

INCLUDING THE HORSE

I grew up in a riding culture that was all about making horse do things. Make them canter, make them stand still, make them go faster, make them put their head down. Considering that we "loved" horses, there was a lot of forcing going on. A lot of ignoring how the horse felt about everything. My horse Caleb was expected to play by human rules, but the only way he found out what those rules was by breaking them.

This went on for years. No wonder he bucked unexpectedly. Now I see it as his way to let me know about his confusion. Bucking was the only way he could get my attention.

In my late twenties, I became not only frustrated by my gelding's behavior, but also by my own lack of knowledge about how to fix it. Plus, it didn't feel good to bully him into something he didn't want to do. Using my legs and hands as weapons made me feel horrible about what I was doing to him.

Caleb had a dark spot on his otherwise pink muzzle, right between his nostrils. At first, I would gently touch this area, marveling at the dark outer color against the delicate pink of his white nose. After a while, when no one was looking, I would gently kiss that dime-sized spot. I've met horses who didn't like this up-close-and-personal face contact, but Caleb wasn't one of them. I started to wonder if he and I could experience this sweetness when I rode him, too.

I thought I was heartbroken when Caleb went lame the second year into our dressage training. I soon figured out, however, that mostly what I was feeling was relief. As I gave him extra care and he got better, we started going on short trail rides. I rode bareback through the pine and cinder hills in the evenings, appreciating the sunsets and the winding down of a day. I kicked less and felt the stirrings of gratitude more. It crossed my mind that my horse was far more forgiving than most people I knew. Including myself.

Several years and three horses later, I was attending a clinic when I heard Mark explain the idea of including your horse in whatever it was you wanted to do. I'd been experimenting with the idea of asking my horses to do things, but looking back, I was asking with an undercurrent of "You'd better say 'yes.'" Force is force, no matter how it's disguised.

I now see that including our horse, and asking our horse to participate in whatever crazy human activity we have in mind for the day, is a lifelong art. It's made up of setbacks and mistakes, triumphs and transformations. It's also made up of muddy boots, hay-filled pockets, and the gentle whuffing of a velvet muzzle against your cheek.

"Asking" is seeking consent. "Including" is welcoming the answer. And if the answer doesn't match up to our vision, we figure out why that is, and then ask a different way. Maybe we need to breathe more. Maybe we need to move in the saddle less. Maybe we need to take the horse's advice and slow things down for a moment.

The first ride I had after that clinic, as I put Caleb's bareback pad on, I thought, *We're going for a trail ride.* Although Caleb was prone to bouts of bucking and liked to run really fast, he was mostly a quiet and cheerful horse. That whole ride, when I thought about what I'd like to do with him—when I thought about us, about how we could do something together—there was a change in both of us that I didn't register until later. I'd finally experienced what was meant by the word "connection."

As riders, if we aren't careful, we can become the literal embodiment of the saying, "Just along for the ride." Asking and including our horses in our thoughts establishes a certain quality of connection that forcing and pushing won't ever replicate. Our horse may be going through the motions on the outside, but her inside will be firmly shut away. A horse who feels safe (not surprisingly, the idea of inclusion resonates with a herd animal) is a horse who will show us her true and full heart.

LEAVING DOUBT OUT OF THE SADDLE

I'd already been an instructor for two decades in 2008. All of my clients until then were women who loved their horses. Lessons were often a lively discussion of ideas and sharing information about the horse that the owner had brought. Many lessons were also a time to share the deep vulnerability of the rider's doubts. Often, it was helping reassure them that they were on the right track, or that we could help them find the right track if they felt lost. I had great admiration that the riders who came to us trusted us not only with their horse, but their personal concerns too.

That same summer, at a weeklong clinic Mark and I were teaching, for the first time ever all the clinic participants were men. Some were clean-shaven, some had a mustache, one had a brown beard shot through with gray. All were wearing cowboy hats for shade from the hot sun of a July day in Colorado.

I didn't give it a second thought, figuring this clinic would go pretty much the same as every other weeklong clinic we've ever taught. Our clinics were—and still are—mostly attended by women. This week of having all guys stands out in my memory.

After our brief Monday morning discussion, we went to get our horses and saddle them.

Throughout the day, I'd ride up to one of the men and ask him how things were going. Often, he'd ask a question that I'd do my best to answer. I'd watch as he made the adjustment with his horse, smiled and said, "Thanks," and rode away.

This happened the whole day. My teaching was measured in minutes, not hours.

As Mark and I drove home, I wondered why I hadn't been teaching like I usually did. My conclusion was that these guys were getting to know us, and it was first-day jitters. Or maybe it was me—maybe I was a little nervous, teaching so many guys when for all of my teaching career, I'd worked with women.

On Tuesday morning we had another short meeting. Another hot day. Another day where I talked for no more than one hour in an eight-hour period.

As Mark drove our big work truck up the canyon in the cooling evening, my thoughts took a different and less attractive tone: *These guys don't like me. Don't respect me. Have a problem with women and will only go to the guy for help. What's their problem? Do I suck as an instructor?*

During our Wednesday morning meeting, the guys are a bit chattier. There's laughter and a general feeling of ease around the picnic table in the hay barn. We are now used to one another and used to the heat.

After saddling my horse, I ride out to the field, ready to teach. I approach one guy at a time, or a guy approaches me. We chat about their question. Again, they try out my suggestion a couple of times and ride away to work on what they learned.

During our drive through the canyon that evening, I vented to Mark that in three days, I had done less talking that I ever had in my teaching life. Was he teaching a lot? Talking a lot? Mark smiled. "No more than usual, I guess."

By Thursday afternoon, I had solved the source of my confusion. These guys got the information they needed, worked with it, then moved on to the next thing. While they obviously cared about their horses and enjoyed spending time with them, they got on, they rode, and they asked questions when questions came up.

There wasn't a lag time between a horse's action and their response, mostly because they weren't questioning or doubting either their skill or the information they received.

Before I take this topic any further, I want to emphasize that I'm *not* saying men are better equestrians than women. I'm not saying *all* men learn like this, or that *all* women have the same responses while learning. I'm speaking in generalities and, of course, there are many ways that all genders take in and respond to the world.

My big "a-ha" moment with these guys was when I realized that having any answer to a horse's question is better than having no answer. Self-doubt—or any doubt—doesn't have to sit in the saddle with us. Since I've worked with mostly women during my teaching career, addressing conscious or unconscious doubt during a lesson happened frequently. Doubt is the most common mindset that interferes with our ability to respond to our horse when they need us to. This was the first layer of realization after the clinic with all men.

Nearly a decade later, I've also realized that it exemplifies the roles women and men are raised to take on, and how dealing with horses often reflects the ideas we were brought up with. That women (myself included) doubt themselves so easily points to a weak spot in our culture. While I believe this is changing, and more of us are rejecting these kinds of stereotypical gender roles, I've become much more committed to providing a horse person of any gender ways to feel more confident when they're with their horse. How to develop a mindset that provides answers and is more ok with mistakes.

While gender roles and their effects on each of us aren't the topics of this book, I mention them as a way to suggest that it's useful to consider how we might be with our horses that move beyond entrenched ideas about our gender. Or perhaps false beliefs about who we are.

When we're with horses, it's time to be clear and consistent.

Time to take a deep breath with confidence and ask for what we'd like. When we're away from horses, we can think and process because we're the only one searching for an answer.

I believe we are all capable of giving our horse what they need from us in the moment: listening, heart, understanding, clarity, and kindness.

The rest of that week, I laughed along with the guys, and smiled with them at a job well done.

I have a hunch they had no idea that I was the one who learned as much, if not more, than they did. I learned that it really isn't about gender. It certainly isn't about strengthening the habit of doubting ourselves.

What matters to horses, and to our learning process, is that we don't let doubt get in the saddle with us, and that we come up with an answer, even if we make mistakes. Coming up with an answer is an active form of learning. Making mistakes helps us home in on an answer that will best serve our horse, or the situation we find ourselves in. No matter our gender, our horse will always appreciate a clear answer to her questions.

SHEDDING A HEAVY COAT

As spring approaches, our horse Rocky is so itchy that he rubs up against pine trees to scratch the hair off. I take the shedding brushes out to his paddock and spend time reaching all the parts he can't. He's an old horse now, and, like many of us, is sprouting hair where there didn't used to be any. However, this hair is thick and grips like winter is moments away.

I've written a lot about the importance of remaining calm in the midst of chaos. During the coronavirus pandemic, the chaos waits for us every day. We see that the pleasures and places we thought would always be there no longer are. We watch the numbers affected by the virus go up. No one knows where this train stops. Or even pauses.

As much as anyone can, I've tried to stay informed without spinning emotionally out of control. Many of my loved ones are far away, and some of them are older. We live in a mountain town that depends on tourism. We're self-employed, but—concerned about our students' safety, and our own—cancelled our early-spring clinics. Thousands of people have lost loved ones, and thousands more are ill. My hamster brain runs itself ragged on the coronavirus wheel.

As horse people, we know that one of the skills required to

thrive with horses is the ability to maintain a level head. This is more important than any technique.

So, when I went out to brush the horses that morning, I was aware how close I was to full-blown anxiety. I was also aware that I was relying on my practices to keep me grounded. Deep breath in. Slow breath out. Listen to the birds. Feel the sun warming skin that hasn't felt the air on it in months.

The most powerful moment of revelation came when I was brushing Rocky and watching his obvious pleasure at being relieved of a winter coat that had become too heavy. I was fascinated by the ssshhhshhhing of the brush and the wads of hair released and fallen to the ground. Rocky stood still even while I brushed those sensitive and hard-to-reach places—the inside of his hind legs, the underside of his round belly.

The sun, warm. The air, warm. The birds singing. Rocky, his head down, sighing in relief.

The pandemic coat is heavy, too. If we believe we wear it alone, it can feel suffocating. But we aren't alone, are we? We have each other, and we are all wearing the same coat. We may need to socially distance, but we can still smile be kind to others. We can leave supplies for neighbors who need them. If we are able to sew, we can make face masks. We can volunteer to deliver meals to those who can't get out. Even during a time of such stress and fear and tragedy, we can find ways to focus our mind and heart toward being part of a solution.

Our knowledge of the earth, the air, the sea, and the skies is built on thousands of years of exploration and multiple layers of bravery and courage exercised by those who have gone before us. Horsemanship is the same: What we know, we know because someone else either tried and failed or tried and succeeded. I believe horses themselves are doing their part to help us become better listeners and, ideally, better people on this planet we share with so many other forms of life.

I take comfort in nature's offerings, working to be in each moment and enjoy her beauty, even the beauty of a horse's winter hair on the ground and the promise of a shiny coat. I take comfort in all the people who got us where we are today. I feel gratitude for people we will never know or meet, working together to solve our historically unique crisis. However this turns out, I also have faith that we will learn things that future generations will use to further their own lives. We may even learn something about ourselves, both individually and collectively, that changes us.

The knowledge and understanding we've collected about horses over the years can serve us well. Just when we think we can't bear anymore, we think of that horse who seemed "broken," and how, with kindness and patience, he came back. How the simple act of mindful breathing can help us through our day. How focusing on the way horses ruffle air through their nostrils, or the wild grassiness of their smell, provides a moment of rest in a world that's anything but restful.

Those lessons aren't just platitudes or things with which to distract ourselves. They can be applied right now as we weather this storm. Really, we may no longer have the luxury of *not* applying them.

We brush our horses. Listen to them munch hay. Ground ourselves in the present so firmly that for a few moments, we are unencumbered by heavy coats and can bask in the warm spring air. Weave enough of those moments together and we might actually be able to feel something other than dread. By taking off that coat, we can experience the simple pleasure of sunshine on our bare arms.

TRUSTING OURSELVES

Trust can be a complicated thing.

For the past decade, I have been working on learning how to trust myself. Trust is what I realized I was gaining during the years I trained in the martial art of Aikido. As my confidence in my ability to protect myself grew, so did my trust in myself. Aikido taught me how to most effectively use my body in falls and rolls; a plus each time I came off a horse, which, by the way, was always due to rider error.

Trust also informs my work as a riding instructor. I trust that I will be able to help a horse and a person so that at the very least, they feel better. I trust myself to handle a myriad of situations. I also trust myself to communicate effectively so that what I'm trying to share gets across. I don't get it right all the time, but a foundation of trusting myself to handle most things has brought an internal peace of mind.

Where does our friend the horse fit into this "trust" thing? Many training techniques do a good job of working with the ways horses learn, and most involve gaining a horse's trust. But I think we mistake a lot of what horses do as reflections of their trust—or lack of—in us.

Not that they are incapable of feeling trust, or of being trustworthy. But on a day-to-day basis, I believe, horses are just looking to get along. They will do what they're asked the best they know how in order to get through another day in what must be to them quite a wacky place.

Compliance is not the same as trust.

As a trainer and instructor, I'm fortunate to be in a position to witness, experience, and feel some amazing breakthroughs between horses and their humans. I hear many stories from folks who have experienced things with their own horses that are powerful and beautiful and wild and unexplainable. I have similar stories as well.

I've discovered that unless you trust yourself—who you are, what you do, the choices you make, and how you shape your life—you cannot truly trust anyone else, human or horse included.

Humans and horses are, after all, going to be and do and say and act in unpredictable ways. When we trust ourselves, what others do or say doesn't have quite the traction it might otherwise exert. As I work on increasing my self-trust, my requirement that others show up as absolutely trustworthy (which I now know means predictable) has softened.

I don't believe we can ever fully, truly, empirically know what is going on inside another creature—human, horse, sparrow, or jellyfish. We can make educated guesses based on patterns of behavior or, in our own species' case, dialogue, and we can feel things energetically, a kind of "knowing but not knowing how you know." But absolutely, positively know? Probably not.

Asking a horse to trust us and having him do it is one of the pinnacles of horsemanship for good reason: they're very large animals with one of the fastest reaction times on the planet. They're also powerful and can move in several directions—occasionally at the same time. A trusting horse is usually a calmer horse and by definition, a safer horse to ride and be around.

Sometimes, though, in our pursuit of that cloud-hidden peak, I think we get into a bit of a rut. We measure ourselves and sometimes our horses, by how trusting they are or aren't. It becomes this nagging worry: Does my horse trust me? How can I get my horse to trust me more? What do I need to do, who do I need to see, how do I need to ride, how can I better take care of my horse? You get the idea. Pretty soon, it spins off into unpredictable places, places that bog us down. Where do we go once we're at a standstill?

As humans, we're incredibly focused on externals. It's only when we take time to examine what lives inside us that we find gaps in our own trust of ourselves. It's understandable that gaining a horse's trust can be an affirmation, a way to bridge a gap we may have in trusting ourselves. Who hasn't felt better because a horse gave us something, and then felt better again when we gave something back?

When we are around our horse and there is mutual trust, there is a palpable sense of heart expansion. Of feeling that all is well. Even if the rest of our life is crumbling around our manure-crusted boots, being in the presence of a horse can reassure us and give us a place to feel the ground under our feet. A renewed sense of strength.

But even this good stuff can create a place where pressure builds. We put pressure on ourselves to achieve that goal and we inadvertently put pressure on the horse to start trusting. It may be a subtle or quiet pressure, but it's still pressure.

If we strive to establish trust, if it's our main focus, we sometimes not only miss a bunch of good stuff the horse may offer, but also, may mistake compliance, dissociation, or lack of movement for trust. Then, when things go haywire—or as my UK friends like to say, "pear-shaped"—we have no idea what happened.

Here's the bare bones of what I've learned about this: If I focus on how I can more fully trust myself, whether my horse trusts me or not becomes less of an urgent issue. This, in turn, reduces the pressure on both of us. I would like my horse to feel good about what we're doing. I'd like her to understand it fully. I'd like her to be physically and mentally comfortable.

But whether she trusts me or not isn't up to me. That's a state each horse (or human) must come to by themselves. Whether it's self-achieved or granted us by our horse, trust is a way of going through our lives. It can't be forced. The guardianship of the trust the horse gives us, just like the guardianship of trust in ourselves, is a daily practice.

I believe that if the horse feels good about our interactions, then so do I. I intend to spend the rest of my days finding out how to behave so that I create the least interference with a horse's capacity to feel quieter, more at peace, and less worried about life in general.

ACCEPTANCE OR RESIGNATION?

Videos of horses being taken advantage of or treated harshly bring up a lot of anger in me. In one sense, the anger is irrational; I don't know the situation, the person, or the horse. Therefore, my anger is based on a ton of illogical leaps.

In another sense, when I know how bright and hot horses can shine? How grounding it is to be included in that brightness? When I see a dullness in these horses' eyes, in their bodies, in their lack of response to their environment, I get angry.

Others who love horses get angry, too. If the video or photo is on social media, they might be angry enough to write a comment, or chastise the person publicly. So far, so standard. But what happens next is a battle that gets further and further away from horses and deeper and deeper into the territory of proving we're right.

Anything we believe in, horse-related or not, we hold close, and when we see something that runs into that belief, it's difficult to shrug it off. In any event, shrugging it off isn't the most effective form of action.

So we when we see a horse being badly treated, it feels like we have two options: get in a fight about it, knowing that the likelihood of changing the other person's mind is zero to not ever, or pretend we didn't see it.

I've always considered myself to be an accepting person. After a lot of years of internal digging what I discovered is that I'm actually more comfortable with resignation than with acceptance.

Acceptance has a vibrant quality to it; acceptance is a light and airy house that the sun and breeze can move through freely.

Resignation, on the other hand, is a dark, stale place. Not much grows there or thrives.

When I think about the potential for horses to be themselves, in all their power and wisdom, and then see photos or videos of horses who are the exact opposite, it strikes me that they've become the equine equivalent of a dull and worn-out human. Resignation isn't just a human trait. I see it in horses who've been badly handled as well.

What's the most useful response? Be a crusader? Be an example? Keep quiet and focus on taking care of our own horse? I believe the answer is a balance in all three. Acceptance is knowing that the only way the lives of horses will improve is if we educate ourselves, share our knowledge appropriately, and take meaningful actions to support those who are also improving horse's lives.

One way to do that—a way I personally practice, although not as much as I'd like—is to support nonprofit horse rescues and sanctuaries whose work I believe in. In my home state of Colorado, we've been involved with one of them, Happy Dog Ranch, for more than a decade. Happy Dog Ranch is a sanctuary with a dedicated volunteer staff and therapists who offer equine-assisted therapy. Property owners John and Bernadette provide each horse in their care with a safe and supportive place to live out their lives. It's one of our favorite places to work and visit.

The Pegasus Project in Texas does the heartbreaking work of rescuing horses who have been starved, beaten, and abused. The kind of horses they're not sure can be saved, but are willing to put their heart and soul into trying. Most of the time, the horse not only lives, but thrives and can be placed in a loving home. Then there are those who can't. In that situation, Allison and Mike and their incredible team give the horse a peaceful and dignified death. Pegasus's open-door policy is broad and inclusive, and I'm happy to write them a check. If we all did a little, a lot would get done.

The other action-based thing I do is to help people not only feel better about their interactions with horses but also, do better as well. Sharing knowledge and understanding goes a long way toward feeling like I'm pitching in to make life better for horses.

Horses are easy: show them what you'd like, and while they may or may not understand, they'll try their heart out to accommodate it. People? That's another matter. In order for the horse to feel better, I have to find a way into the person's way of looking at the world to help them with whatever they feel is important. How I say things, the order I say things, and the words and tone of voice I use all contribute to the other person's willingness to hear what I'm saying, to make it their own and share that softer way with their horse. Or not. Sometimes there are no "right" words or "right" tones. People are such a mystery.

Which sets us up for the next level of choosing resignation or acceptance: What happens when we give our best and it's not enough? When we show up with our best selves and the horse, or person, or situation still goes off the rails?

My mom once said, "Sometimes, you do everything right, and it all still falls apart. That's life."

Personally, this is the exact situation that will cause me to think about staying in bed for a week, whimpering into my flannel sheets. But what I actually do is allow myself a few hours of feeling bad. Then I'll go for a walk with the dogs, eat some dark chocolate, and find a way to affirm that some things are bigger than us and require lots of people's best efforts, not just mine.

This is also a way of making things better for horses. We do our part. We do our best on any given day. We encourage, educate, and cheer for people who are working at being better, not only for their horses, but for themselves as well. Then we let them walk the path they've chosen as we continue on our own.

It's such a relief to truly understand that it isn't my responsibility to fix the world, merely do my part. At this point in my life, that feels like enough to be going on with.

If you'd like more information about the horse rescues mentioned here, you can visit:

Happy Dog Ranch
happydogranch.org/

The Pegasus Project
www.mypegasusproject.org/

THE WHOLE HORSE

It was a cloudy morning as I chatted with Jaycee about what she'd like to work on with her horse Scamp.

"I've been making him move his feet because everyone I've worked with says he needs to move his feet more. But he's always spooky," Jaycee said.

I thought about this for a moment and then replied, "When you say, 'make him move his feet,' what do you mean?"

"Well, this is what I do." She picked up the end of her lead rope, spun it quickly at Scamp's nose, and stepped aside as he took off to the end of the line and then bounced around in a circle before settling into a stiff lope.

"Okay," I said. "When you say that it's important for a horse to move, you're right. But if we just focus on his feet and not how we're asking him to move or the quality of that movement, we're missing a big part of the picture."

Jaycee nodded and pulled on the line so Scamp would stop. He planted his feet in the dirt, raised his head, and snorted.

I continued explaining. "Moving feet can be a tricky way to think of this. If we only focus on the feet and not how the horse is feeling inside his own skin, we may miss helping him reach the point of relaxation. The feet are a way in, not the end goal. Let's present him with the option of moving on a circle more softly, and let's also watch for his breathing to become regular and his movement to relax."

I showed her how to step out of Scamp's way. We talked about how to breathe more deeply and how to use the end of her rope farther away from his body. We started with a slow twirl. Scamp looked at the rope, then burst into a fast trot.

"That was better than running away," I said. "Now, keep breathing and relax your body a little."

Scamp trotted a couple more laps before he, too, took a breath and slowed to a walk.

"Let's change how we ask him to stop. I'd like you to stand still as you exhale. If Scamp isn't able to stop with that, we can use the lead rope to ask."

Scamp walked a half-circle before drifting to a halt. He shook his head and neck, exhaled, and stood quietly.

"Wow," said Jaycee. "That was really different. He's starting to relax."

I nodded. "Yes. That's the inside of the horse releasing tension. My hunch is that once we turn the volume down for both of you, he'll be able to not only move his feet, but you can help him feel more relaxed as well."

The phrase "move their feet" is ingrained in the fabric of horse culture.

On the one hand, it's great that so many people have learned this phrase. On the other, it can lead to tunnel vision—or maybe I should say hoof vision—about what it is we're trying to accomplish with our horse.

We can sometimes get so caught up in "moving the feet" that we forget that doing so is the external result of an internal process. When a horse feels pressure or tension and needs to move, that energy reaches the feet last. But something causes that need to move. We can use the energy of movement to get back to the inside of the horse in a way that will help him calm down.

We aren't moving the feet to punish the horse or wear him

out. We're allowing the horse to do what horses are designed to do: move. A whole-body, inside-and-out process is expressed *through* the feet, not *by* them.

Moving the feet isn't a part of "making the wrong thing difficult and the right thing easy" either, since horses don't know what the wrong or right thing is anyway. Horses look for what brings them comfort and ease. Their tolerant natures seek quiet places. Sometimes they need to move a lot to find that quiet place. But if we focus only on moving their feet without regard for the rest of them, I have a hunch that the movement can feel punishing instead of relieving.

By the end of the lesson, Jaycee and Scamp were able to work together quietly. Scamp could walk, trot, and lope on a relaxed circle. He was breathing better, his body was loose, and he had stopped being hyper-alert.

In the end, it wasn't his feet that needed our attention. It was the horse himself.

YOUR HORSE ASKS
THIS QUESTION

After holding a horse brain at a recent seminar, I felt like I'd been on the emotional equivalent of a roller coaster. After swooping down from heights of awe that holding a horse's brain sent me to, and then climbing another rise as I learned about brain anatomy, by the last day I felt saturated in knowledge.

The seminar, given by Dr. Steve Peters, PsyD, ABN, Diplomate in Neuropsychology, focused on equine brain anatomy—which regions control which responses, and a beginner's guide to neurochemicals and how they control horses' responses and reactions.

After learning the science behind horse behavior, a lot of ideas I'd had floating around suddenly made sense. One of the biggest connections I made was that horses are constantly monitoring their environment. What we call "distraction" is actually a way for them to answer their question, "Am I safe."

When we jokingly say that our horse has ADD, what we're actually saying is that we're allowing her to remain in a state of disconnection from both herself and us. Horses didn't evolve to be in a constant state of high alert. In a herd, watching out for danger is a shared duty; some horses sleep while others stay awake. Some horses eat while others look out for predators. There's an ebb and flow to relaxation and being alert, for standing still and eating, for moving along to the next destination.

So when we have a horse who is seemingly nervous all the

time and can't settle with us or focus on the work we'd like to do, the first question we ask is why. The answer often starts with a horse being physically uncomfortable. A compromised horse is an easier target for a predator, so it makes sense that she would need to be more alert.

It's also very common for humans to bring on a state of high alert. If we've not learned how to be with a horse in a way that encourages focus and relaxation, horses will come to associate us with "I'd better watch out," which then becomes the way the horse operates.

Horses have a highly responsive and very fast system for answering that constant question, "Am I safe?" You might say that horses have a built-in radar that makes ours look like it runs in slow motion.

When horses detect something they think might endanger their lives, the response takes what's called the low road. For example, the sight of a wildly flapping flag goes from the eyes to the brain's thalamus and directly into the amygdala (the center for fight or flight). This process takes milliseconds. As horse people, we know a lot can happen in those milliseconds.

To put that in perspective, our average reaction time to something we see is 250 milliseconds, and 170 milliseconds to something we hear. For horses, the visual reaction happens in 180 to 200 milliseconds, and the aural, in 140 to 160 milliseconds. However you understand the numbers, horses respond more quickly to their environment than we do.

Horses constantly monitor everything going on around them. They can't turn their senses off and on like we do, with our selective seeing. (If you'd like to know more about how our brain filters out information, look up "inattentional blindness.")

Building an understanding with the horse is a process of encouraging their curiosity instead of their fear. Curiosity allows and fosters learning. Any time a horse fears for his life, he's not learning. Until the safety question is answered, a horse will continue to use every sense he has to figure out whether to stay or leave. Whether to relax or flee.

If we keep things relatively quiet and provide clear guidance about what we're looking for, the horse will come back. When we do our best to answer the horse's primary question, he's able to switch over to his natural curiosity and learn more effectively.

It has occurred to me that the only time horses are fully "paying attention" is when they're on the verge of fleeing. We've all seen our horse zero in on something before deciding to quickly leave. What we call "paying attention" may actually be troublesome for our horses.

So much of horse training feels narcissistic: We want both their eyes, we want their head turned in our direction, we want all of their attention, we want their full body to be at our beck and call. We want to be the center of their universe.

Being with horses gets a lot easier if we share, instead of hijacking and demanding. Of course, there are days when I can't give my full attention to anything. Who am I to insist that others, including horses, do it for my benefit?

So when a horse looks off into the distance or can't seem to "focus," it's never bothered me. I never really understood what the ruckus of "having their attention" was about. Until I learned about their internal radar recently, I probably wasn't bothered because I did the same thing myself: when overwhelmed and unable to escape, I looked away and went somewhere else.

Those who have been preyed upon by another human have a particular set of experiences and way of viewing the world that allow them to viscerally understand the horse's primal need for safety. I've spent my adult life evaluating every situation I find myself in, where the exits are, who's around me, and how I can escape if I need to. Or fight. All of this is almost subconscious.

For me, accepting horses for who they are means continuing to learn about them instead of relying on hearsay. Accepting our horse means we find ways of working with him that encourage that feeling of safety.

This doesn't mean we do nothing. It means that education/training with a horse goes a lot more smoothly if we are educated, too. If we understand the basic mechanics of what makes a horse tick, we're far less likely to get frustrated or take it out on our horse.

Instead of saying our horse is "distracted," we could see what horses do as gathering information. Or seeking comfort. Or both. The best-case scenario is that our horse transfers that feeling of safety to us, and that the relationship we have with them meets their need for safety most of the time.

If we can help the horse feel safe, we are safer. If our horses feel safe with us, the chances of accidents, misunderstandings, and miscommunication get lower.

Beyond all this science, understanding more about the horse equals a better life for each horse which whom we come into contact.

YOU CAN BE YOU

Have you ever watched someone do something with their horse and thought, "That will never be me." Or, even worse, had a trainer, experienced horse person, or complete stranger tell you, in so many words, the same thing? As they say in the South, "Bless their heart."

After posting what I thought was an innocuous and positive blog, I got some online feedback from a stranger that felt like a personal attack. The voice that likes to tell me I'm a fraud roared back to life. Private fears thrown in your face are hard to handle.

I can handle differences of opinion. Criticism, even. But in a few sentences, this person crossed that line and made it personal.

I know it got under my skin because when I thought about writing another blog entry, I felt like I'd swallowed a bowling ball. I'm familiar with that weight—I carried it around like an expensive handbag after winding up in the hospital following a horse accident.

However, I also belong to an amazing writer's group. I've never met most of them, but we all know what it's like to write, either publicly or privately. We're all familiar with the I'm-a-fraud fear.

When I went to my fellow writers with the feedback I'd received, looking for ways to stand up after the punch in the gut, I got an outpouring of support. And humor. By the end of the day, I was laughing about it. My husband, who's also a writer, reassured and stood up for me. I went back and read all the comments I get from people who enjoy the blog. I reread my writer's group comments. I spent the next few days focusing on what was working and felt good, especially when that shady devil voice showed up inside my head and said: "You're a fraud, and now everyone knows it." After a while, the voice retreated. Yet, I was relieved that I wouldn't need to write again for a month.

Then, there I was, a month later, my handbag of fear clutched to my chest. What better way to exorcise this demon than writing about the very thing the small, rolled-up-in-a-hole part of me would rather keep to myself?

When it comes to anything we feel passion for whether it's horses, climbing trees, or baking, sharing that passion can be nerve-wracking. We know what it's like to be human, to stumble and maybe even fail. As well as amazing kindness and goodness, we also have the capacity to be unkind, thoughtless, critical, and mean.

Sharing talents and passions is an act of courage and extreme optimism. It's saying that we won't bow before criticism (bless its heart), we won't yield to another's judgment or sometimes even our own, and we certainly won't stop what we're doing.

So if you see another horse and rider and feel the need to say, "That will never be me," celebrate that. Because it won't ever be you. *You* can only be you, and your expression of horsemanship is uniquely between you and your horse. You know yourself and your horse best. You know what feels right and good, and what doesn't. I think a lot of us get hung up on trusting ourselves. But there comes a time when trusting who we are is the only choice we have.

When and if the thought "That will never be me," arises, try this. If you hear or think something that stings, find five things that don't. Or conversely, remember my favorite bumper sticker: "Don't believe everything you think." Talk to your friends; I bet they have a lot of ways to move beyond hurt feelings. Look in your horse's soft and kind eyes; there isn't anything there but an appreciation of who you are. Every time that shady devil shows, go back to the good stuff. Go back to your horse.

A SAFE PLACE

When we drove up to the horses' paddock, Rocky and Rusty were lying down taking a nap together in the warm morning sun. They looked at us through half-open eyes; they had old hay on their faces and their lower lips were droopy and lined with dirt. It appeared that we woke them up out of a sound sleep.

They chose the warmest and softest part of their paddock, where the dirt has mixed with wind-blown hay and dried-out manure that's been walked on and rolled in. This must be the equine version of a memory-foam mattress.

When we let the dogs out of the truck, Rusty got up first and stood by Rocky as he raised himself on his front legs, rocked forward and then got his wobbly hind end straightened out. Rocky has been lame since February, and after two very thorough vet visits, we know what it isn't, but not what it is. The good news is that it's nothing horrible—no broken bones, no hock or stifle issues.

I've written about Rocky a lot. He's now twenty-two and we've had him for all but the first seven of those years. In all that time, he's never been sick or lame. He's level-headed in a herd, which means he doesn't get into fights and doesn't injure himself. He helped me regain my eroded confidence after a bad horse accident. He's always ready to work, cheerful, and easy to be around.

Rusty, the most aggressive horse that we've brought into our herd, has decided that Rocky is his best pal. When no one else in the herd can move Rusty, Rocky can, and often does.

When another horse decides to move Rocky, Rusty rushes in and drives the other horse off. They share their feed, they stand head to tail in the summer swishing flies, and apparently, they nap together as well. Moving like an eight-legged horse (though one of those legs has a noticeable drag), the duo relaxes in each other's company.

When we got Rusty in 2015, he wasn't a happy horse. As we've taken care of him and listened to what he was saying to us, he's calmed down and shown himself to be not only reliable (as in, my ten-year-old niece could ride him by herself) but also very sweet.

This spring, while we were quarantined at home, one of my favorite things to do was to watch our herd as we did barn chores. When I watch these two chestnut geldings rest in one another's company, it gives me much to think about in terms of friendship. Whether it's a happy human friendship or a quiet horse friendship, there are ingredients we can include in our interactions with horses that mimic both. There are ways that horses bond with each other that aren't difficult for us to replicate.

We can be as consistent as possible in all our interactions with them. We can offer energy without a lot of emotion behind it. We can spend time together that doesn't always involve doing something.

While horses aren't confused by a large amount of energy, what does disturb them and interrupt that consistency we aim for, is energy with emotion. That means if we are trying to do something with a horse and become frustrated or angry and then add the anger to the equation, the horse will likely try to put distance between us, get more agitated herself, or shut down and wait for things to mellow out.

Assuming there's plenty to eat and horses don't have to fight for food, the reason horse herds are quiet is because they each know where another horse can and cannot be pushed. Even if that other horse is explosive with their boundaries, other horses don't worry about him because they know where the boundary is. They make sure not to cross it. Nothing is personal with Rusty. He doesn't want anyone but Rocky next to him. He doesn't get "mad" at the other horses. All of his energy is only that; no emotion involved.

Imagine if a horse's boundary changed every day. Or even minute to minute. That must feel as though there's a bomb in the herd, only no one knows what will light the fuse. Some people hesitate to use the word "friendship" when it comes to a horse preferring one herd mate over another. I have no such hesitation. Even though a friendship between horses looks different than a friendship between humans, some of the rules aren't that much different.

Before we put the dogs back in the truck to head home, I glanced at the paddock where Rusty and Rocky were eating side by side. Their eyes were closed, their bodies were relaxed. I couldn't have asked for a clearer picture of what a horse feels like when he's in a safe place.

HORSE AS A RIVER

Life has a way of answering questions in ways that are completely surprising. It took a horse falling on me to understand that "resistance" is a completely human concept.

I get it. I know that horses do things because they don't understand, because they're avoiding or experiencing pain, because they're afraid or worried or tired. If we see resistance in a horse, it's because we've brought it on and are interpreting it in the only way we, as humans, understand. For horses, there is no such thing as "resistance." None.

The delicious thing about this horsemanship journey we chose is the opportunity to experience the world through the eyes and responses of a different species. Instead of trying to make the horse more human, I believe the adventure lies in us choosing to be more horse.

Horses, like water, will almost always flow along the path of least resistance. They're the stream and we're the rocks around which they flow. I've felt and witnessed many beautiful moments when horse and human blend their movements and become a free-flowing river, a living picture of harmony. And isn't that one of the many reasons we love horses—to get out of ourselves, and see the world from their perspective?

So, if horses choose the path of least resistance, yet do things that, to us, are unexpected or contrary to our wishes, what's going on?

Here's an example: A rider asks her horse to go from walk to trot. There's a tail swish, a pin of the ears, and an abrupt transition after the rider applies a lot of force with her legs. Once in the trot, it is rough, without rhythm, and the horse keeps trying to get back to the walk while the rider uses leg pressure to keep him in a trot.

Again, if we feel what we would call "resistance," it is because we are bringing it to the horse. Either our bodies (the outside) or our emotions/thoughts/intent (the inside) close and create a sort of roadblock the horse now has to get around—the rock in the stream. Usually riders, either through learned habit or unintentionally, will tighten their bodies in preparation for the transition. This tightening usually starts in the lower back and shoulders and spreads to the extremities. Then, their whole body locked, they say "go faster!" to the horse. Basically, what this does is send two separate and distinct messages to the horse, who now has to stiffen his body in response to our stiffness but move forward at the same time.

The part of us that wants to go from walk to trot (the inside) will sometimes follow our body. In other words, our focus goes from "my horse is walking" to "I want my horse to trot." This is the point at which riders will often freeze on the inside, and I've seen it at least a thousand times. The signal is that the rider momentarily stops breathing. I often joke that somewhere, buried in the ancient part of our brain, is a voice saying, "Riding something this big and this fast is *reeeeaally* risky!" (It's only kind of a joke, though.) After talking to many riders and witnessing the many ways they use their bodies in a transition, it seems fair to say that somewhere inside we go from "Let's trot," to "Uh-oh!" to "Whew! That went well," to "Why isn't my horse trotting more smoothly?" This happens, of course, without our being aware of it.

We can also see the disconnect in the way we talk or think about it. We usually focus on what we, as the rider, want the horse to do. There's nothing wrong with this, and we aren't bad people if we fall into this habit. But if we'd like to remove the rocks from the stream, it's helpful to think about how "we"

— my horse and I — can move into a different rhythm, the trot.

Here's another scenario: the rider takes a deep breath in, and exhales while thinking, *We are trotting now*, then applies a cue with her relaxed legs, if needed. The rider keeps this pattern going until she and the horse are doing the same thing (trotting—for the rider, this is keeping a focus on the intention to trot, for the horse, it's actually doing the trotting).

Openness is the opposite of resistance. If we can't present openness to our horse, it's going to make it very difficult for our horse to find it. Our requests become how we open into them, both externally and internally.

What does this all have to do with resistance? We spend a lot of our lives saying "No." Saying "No," is also completely okay; in fact, it's healthy. Resistance is also healthy—think Martin Luther King, Jr.; Rosa Parks; or the Suffrage movement. What I'm speaking of here is our habit of giving a negative answer, or a negative outlook, or a negative thought without examination, almost as a way of life.

If we're not careful, our horsemanship can become a litany of "no" and "don't do that": don't pull on the bit, don't fall in on the circle, don't anticipate me, don't canter when I want a walk, don't pin your ears. This isn't necessarily bad or good, but what it can do is add more rocks to that stream. Add enough rocks, and the stream gets diverted. It goes somewhere else.

What if we instead focused on being more open ourselves, and helping our horse through troublesome spots? It's time to lay to rest the notion that it's us against them. Our horses may be giving us the perfect opportunity to examine such things, which will at the same time help them feel better about what we're doing. Here's another example.

After my horse Bree fell on me, I went to the hospital. A lot of tests were run. Everyone was very kind and caring. But I was scared, and in pain, and drug hazy. Vulnerable. An uncomfortable feeling for most people, and I was no different. For whatever reason, I accepted what the doctors and Mark were telling me and thanked everyone for their care. I couldn't stop voicing my gratitude, even when crying with pain and fear. I couldn't resist because my body and mind were not able.

My tenacious grip on my own independence was the first thing to go. I couldn't resist help because I wasn't in a position to do so. As I got better at accepting help, I noticed a funny thing. Peace of mind. People are generous, and genuinely desire to help others feel better. As I was helped with such generosity, my grip on my belief of "I must do it myself!" loosened. As this part of me loosened, I began to relax. My pain was manageable. I felt happier, at ease, and grateful for all the support people offered me.

That sense of less resistance has continued. Less busy mind, less judgment, less tendency to jump into my comfort zone and defend it. It's not gone, but it's less. And, I have to say, living with less resistance is a pretty okay thing.

When combined with — a desire to help our horse feel better, our own pliability and a commitment to relaxing inside and out will help us become a river that flows easily around the obstacles in its path. This is harmony. This is flow. This is, I believe, the world of the horse.

YOU HAVE TIMING
AND FEEL

As I was brushing our horses one warm day, I noticed that their short summer coats were falling out. On a day edging toward 95 degrees, while I was in a tee-shirt and cropped jeans, our herd was preparing for snowmageddon.

Horses' ability to be ahead of us in so many ways is astonishing. Their timing goes beyond instinctual to almost psychic. I envy their innate talent at moving quickly, and their desire to get along, no matter the circumstances, is a constant reminder that despite what life throws me, I can try and get along, too.

My husband always says horsemanship would be easy if it wasn't for gravity and timing. The older I get and the longer I live with horses, the more that statement gives me a bittersweet laugh.

Gravity, well, because. If you're reading this and you've ridden for any amount of time (by "time" I mean minutes as well as years), you know that coming off a horse is a *when* proposition, not an *if*. I stopped counting the number of times I've come off horses after I hit the double digits.

Timing. The word "feel" is often paired with timing because in a horse-centric world, it seems one cannot exist without the other.

I doubt that horses stand under a shade tree and contemplate how to improve their timing and feel. Horses are the embodiment of these two holy grails of horsemanship. They already are what we strive to achieve in ourselves.

When we think about improving our timing, about improving our relationship, about improving anything we think is lacking about ourselves, a lot of thinking goes on. And on. I've done decades of thinking about horses and how much I wanted to be better at being with them. I've read mountains of books about horses because I thought that the more that I knew, the better my timing and feel would be.

That was like preparing for three-day eventing at the Olympics by watching YouTube videos.

Thinking, as you probably guessed, is the number-one reason our timing often lags. As riders, we're taught that in order to ride well, we must think a lot. But horses are sensorimotor creatures, which means they feel and they move. That's their job description, that's how they come into this world. One look at a horse brain will tell you that they're wired for movement and for using their senses to figure out if/when/how fast they need to go.

Take a look at a human brain and you'll see that we, on the other hand, are wired for thinking. Here's something exciting, though: We have the capacity to develop the timing and the feel that informs it.

Many years ago, when a dressage instructor told me in subtle ways that I couldn't ride, I chose to quit the lessons. I'd been having doubts about it, so it wasn't a far leap. Turns out, my timing on this issue was great; two weeks later, my horse came up three-legged lame and I spent the next two years figuring out how to help him be sound and comfortable.

Timing is getting out of the way a millisecond before a kick lands in your face. Not that this has happened to me.

Timing is also knowing when to give a horse a break from a concentrated lesson, and when to give yourself a break if you feel you're just not getting it.

We're told that timing and feel cannot be taught.

Except, wait—we use feel and timing hundreds of times a day. It's how we eat breakfast without spilling it down the front of our shirt. It's how we drive and don't get into accidents. It's how we throw a ball for our dog or cook a meal for ourselves or hold a baby without dropping her.

By the time most of us reach adulthood, we've mastered thousands of tiny skills that once seemed like big skills. Walking, speaking, running, eating. We forget how, at one time, we were toddling, drooling, gibberish-speaking, wide-eyed love nuggets who spent every day marveling at the wonder of everything.

As horse people, we grew up and discovered that we were, in fact, part horse and transferred our wonder to these creatures of the wind and plains. At first, we toddled about them, unsure where we fit in relation to them, thrown off balance by the swing of their barrel beneath us and the lift of each elegant leg.

Our hearts were thrown off course by their breath and eyes that seemed to see right through us.

So when someone says, "Ya gotta have feel! Ya gotta have timing!" I smile to myself because we already do.

All we gotta have is the awareness of how to best apply it to working with horses. This means, the more we put ourselves in our horse's context, the better attuned we will be to be using our inborn timing and feel.

Granted, they're unlike anything else in our lives. You may be able to force things on horses, but most of us know and seek out the kind of relationship that cultivates space for mutual consent. It's where the beauty is.

If we can have a little bit of confidence in our own innate abilities, and a little bit of a quieter mind, chances are we're going to get along with our horse just fine. Chances are those skills are inside us, just waiting to be acknowledged.

THE ART OF
IMPERFECTION

When I have no idea what to write about, I pretend, for days, that the perfect idea will come to me. I may not know what it is, but if I wait long enough and pay attention, surely it will appear.

How often do we feel this with our horses? We want to wait until we have the perfect solution for addressing an issue. We want to get it right (mostly, for benevolent reasons), we want it to look perfect, and by the way? Please let it not be messy. And please let no one else be watching.

Unlike writing, where I can stare at a blank page while I sip tea, horses prefer immediate guidance. They need a response—any response—and the sooner the better.

We get hung up on giving them the *right* response. The perfect, mistake-free answer. For example, when our horse trots faster than we want, these thoughts may pass through our head:

"Why is he trotting faster?"

"Is he scared?"

"Does my saddle fit?"

"Am I out of balance?"

"What if I'm not feeding him right?"

"Did I give him too much leg? Maybe I need a different trainer."

"I like my trainer."

"But maybe a second opinion would help?"

"I need a second opinion on my arthritis."

"I wonder if there are supplements that help arthritis?"

"I probably shouldn't have had that fourth cup of coffee."

And so on.

We get off-track because we think we don't have the perfect answer for the horse.

Now, part of this is because we are spectacularly talented at rapid-fire thinking and habituated to consistent distraction. Horses counterbalance this by helping us slow down. Take a breath. Reconnect with our internal landscape, the one that resonates with nature's wildness.

In the space it takes for the thought of that fourth cup of coffee to flash across your mind, there's a gap in communication. It's very similar to having a conversation on a cell phone and having the call fail.

"Hello? Can you hear me now?"

Four, five, ten, twenty-six strides later, maybe we let the horse know about that trot that's too fast. But by then, the horse is doing something else. Maybe he's thinking about stopping or cantering, maybe he's feeling the saddle pad rucked up by his withers. It's difficult to say, but what I'm pretty sure of is that while we choose thinking over doing, the horse is connected to himself, not necessarily to you.

This isn't personal. Horses are hardwired to connect, but we have to give them something to connect to.

Living in our brains, sorting, judging, worrying, is a powerful disconnection. The horse is saying "Hello? Anyone out there?" but because we're running like crazy on our mental race track, we don't reply.

Horses don't seem to be fans of one-way conversations. Everything in their environment gives and receives communication of some sort. They've evolved to live with each other and because of each other. The backbone of this coexistence is paying attention to every signal from their herd mates. Whether we know it or not, our horses are doing this with us too; they can't *not* pay attention. The question is, what are we saying? Even if we aren't saying anything, does that means something to our horse?

Before this starts feeling like too much, or too big a responsibility, consider that we're also talking about creatures who can send and receive messages in less time than it takes to blink. Those messages range all the way from unfathomably subtle (I've seen one of our horses move another without as much as an ear twitch), to overtly physical (biting, kicking, and so forth). The miracle of horses is that, as much chatter as we unknowingly send them, they're able to discriminate between and sort out what they need to listen to and what they can let go of.

So, what can we do?

Take a breath. A big, knock-the-dust-off-your-ribs inhale and exhale. Put your hand on your belly and feel your feet in the stirrups. Take another breath. When your horse does something unexpected, have an answer. Maybe it's to turn him in a smaller circle. Maybe you stop doing what you were doing and do something different. Maybe ride a figure eight, or a serpentine. The point is, your horse will tell you if your answer was effective or not. If it was, great! Build on that. If it wasn't, try something else. Or ask someone to help you figure it out. The "right" or "perfect" answer is a mirage. While I admire our intention to do what is right by the horse, there's a whole lot of freedom in letting go of the need for a perfect answer, at the perfect time, with the perfect feel.

One day, Rocky and I were practicing simple lead changes. On a circle to the right, he would pick up a left lead, we would cross through the middle at a trot and pick up a left circle and he would again be on his left lead, and vice versa. Now, to be fair, I was mostly out to have fun, and Rocky was willing. But I wanted us to be balanced. So, we practiced until the correct lead came through.

My mistakes in my own timing and balance taught me a couple of things: First, I know more about Rocky. Second, while I felt confident about cantering, it was time for me to explore the accuracy of that gait. I wouldn't have learned these things had I not decided to explore simple lead changes and had Rocky not been willing. In my search to set us up for the correct lead on a circle, I tried four different ways, none of which worked. But the fifth adjustment? Bingo.

Just like writing, with horses, we have to start to eventually arrive at the answers. However, if we're always thinking of the perfect way to begin, we end up going nowhere. A response—right or wrong—demonstrates listening. Sometimes, it's the feeling of being heard that starts us on the path to change. But, as Benjamin Franklin said, "If you do nothing, you'll never know when you're done."

BURIED BY CUES

"I'd like my horse to spin faster," the young rider named Rachel said. The short-coupled, well- muscled Palomino mare stood in the arena with her eyes half-closed, swishing her tail.

As Rachel turned her horse to trot to the middle of the arena, the summer sun flashed off one of the silver conchos on her saddle, and the mare's golden mane lifted in the breeze. I remember thinking that together, they were like a bit of poetry.

As Rachel gently touched the reins that hung off the embossed silver bit and moved her hand across the mare's neck to the right, the mare stuck her hind feet in the dirt and turned. Slowly. Carefully. As though she had hit a patch of deep, sticky mud.

I watched as they tried the other direction, but now, the mare was almost at a standstill. Rachel kept giving her aids; the rein cue was gentle, but her legs and seat were pushing, as though her horse was a swing that she could make go higher.

As I walked over to them, I asked, "So, is that pretty normal?"

Rachel caught her breath before answering me, relaxing in the saddle as her mare cocked a hind leg and pricked her ears at the sound of a tractor starting up near the arena.

"Let's just say it's become normal. She wasn't like this when I bought her a year ago."

I nodded and asked what her horse's name was.

Rachel smiled and said, "Daisy."

"And do you both go to shows?"

"Yes, reining, which I love! I bought Daisy so we could start competing in bigger shows."

Then we chatted about Daisy's care. I was happy to hear that Rachel scheduled her horse for regular bodywork sessions, and that her saddle had been fitted so it was comfortable for both horse and rider. We talked about Daisy's teeth, and if she had talked to a vet about ulcers. An experienced farrier was shoeing Daisy and her feet looked to be in good condition. Rachel had been very thorough in Daisy's care, and as far as I could tell, there wasn't a physical reason why Daisy couldn't spin like she used to.

"Rachel, can you take Daisy out for a little walk, jog, and then a lope? I'd like to get an idea of how she moves."

As they turned and walked off, I could see that both Daisy and Rachel were relaxed. Daisy wasn't worried about the busy surroundings we were working in that day and Rachel was a beautifully balanced rider. As they began to jog to the right, I could see she was smiling.

After watching their smooth transitions, relaxed gaits, and easy movement, I was puzzled why movement in a smaller circle would be a problem.

There are times during a lesson when I feel like Sherlock Holmes. What's the person telling me? What's the horse telling me? What do those two things together mean? Certain things that horses do fall within a range of normal. Even what we would label "bad" behavior has its roots somewhere.

But when what I know about horses and having a grasp on that range of behavior don't match what I'm seeing, then I know I'm getting ready to learn something. That's when I pay extra attention.

From what I could see, Rachel and Daisy were a good team. They didn't worry about each other, and both were athletic and ready to perform more complicated movements together. Both were healthy and fit. But neither were able to execute a move that, logically, should have been easy.

"That was great! You both look really awesome." They'd earned the praise, and it also gave me time to feel into the situation, to figure out what our next steps were. I was out of the territory of known solutions and into the depths of not-knowing. Realizing that I'll never know everything about horses and people and the alchemy of their togetherness keeps me from sinking into complacency, and I welcome it.

"Can you show me again what happens when you try to do a spin with Daisy?"

Daisy and Rachel stopped, and that was then I saw it. Rachel's shoulders rose; her back locked; her elbows pressed against her ribcage; and her waist, hips, and legs stiffened. While Daisy didn't display an outward acknowledgment of this change in her rider, I saw a mirroring stiffness in her body. A narrowing of her kind eye. A slight swish of her tail. I felt a split-second rush that meant another clue was on its way.

None of Rachel's cues were hard or abrupt. She wasn't punishing her horse with her legs or her reins. And yet, as they tried to circle to their right, Daisy didn't move any faster than before. In fact, she seemed to move even more slowly.

"Can you ask Daisy to spin the other way?"

Rachel threw me a look that plainly said, *You call that a spin?!* but changed directions. Daisy, if possible, went slower.

As Rachel and Daisy walked toward me, I stood in the dust of a late afternoon, working out how to put into words what I was observing.

"Can you tell me how you ask Daisy to spin?" I said.

"Well, there are two things that are super-important. I want Daisy to be forward into the turn, and she needs to stay straight in her body. If I'm going to the right, I bring my left leg into her and my right leg goes back to hold her hindquarters still and drive her forward. I have to keep my shoulders square and my back and pelvis still. I need to bring the left rein onto her neck but keep her straight, and if she doesn't move, I increase the pressure with my right leg and bring my left leg into her body."

I nodded as I listened and was about to ask another question when Rachel continued her explanation.

"I was told I need to wear spurs, and that if she doesn't move fast enough, to bring my leg forward and use the spur on her shoulder to get her to move away. I can also get her to move to the side, crossing the leading leg over the inside leg and driving her into a small circle, and keep making that circle smaller until she's spinning. My legs need to stay active and my rein pressure the same, and I can't ever use the inside rein to help because she will tip her nose and begin to circle like a helicopter blade, and then that will be a bad habit to break."

Rachel was breathless after her explanation, so I gave her a moment, which was also the moment I needed to decide just how to set up my strategy for Rachel and Daisy.

"Tell me how you ask Daisy for a lope."

"That's easy," she said as she settled into her saddle. "I take a big breath and think about loping, and she goes."

"I bet that feels great."

"Yes! Everything with her is like that. She and I are so connected, which is why this spinning thing is so frustrating."

"I bet there's a way you can ask for a spin like you do for a lope."

"Really?" Rachel was excited, but I could hear the same doubt in her voice that I heard in my head. Channeling Sherlock has its scary moments.

"My hunch is that, since Daisy knows how to spin and you know how to spin, what's happening is that you're using too many cues." I said. I went on to explain that when we're teaching a horse a new skill, we start slowly and give a lot of releases. Repeating the skill in a low-pressure way (meaning, we don't succumb to anger, frustration, or trying to rush a horse) allows the horse to couple the cue with the movement we'd like.

Human and horse brains learn better when things are slower. At first, we may need clearer cues—not bigger cues—to help bridge the gap between what the horse already knows and the particular cue that tells the horse that we'd like him to do something a little more specific.

But if we're not careful, we'll keep using the same number of cues and the same pressure even after the horse has the skill in place. This is where we see frustration happen for both horse and rider.

The horse thinks that because the cues aren't letting up, he's doing something wrong, so he tries something different. The rider increases or gets bigger with the cues, and the horse does something different again, or, as in Daisy's case, does it much more slowly.

Sometimes, the rider takes the horse to a different trainer who inevitably has a different way to teach the skill. Now, both horse and rider have to learn a completely new set of cues for the same move. It either works or it doesn't; most of the time, it doesn't. So, we buy a bigger bit or get a crop or wear spurs so we can scare the horse into the movement he already knows how to do.

Rachel had already said she was reluctant to wear spurs. Observing the way she and Daisy were together, I didn't see a need for her to take that step, but what we could do was start using fewer cues, and find a way for Rachel to relax a little.

"Rachel, I'm going to hold on to Daisy, and I'd like you to close your eyes." She gave me another doubtful look but closed her eyes as I reached up to hold the reins.

"I'd like you to visualize you and Daisy loping. What does that feel like in your body?"

Rachel was silent a moment and as her shoulders dropped down, she said, "I'm relaxed. I know we're taking care of each other and I can feel how much Daisy likes to move. I'm sitting balanced, and I like the wind in my face."

"Okay! That's a great image. Open your eyes and let's chat about that spin again. Here's what I'd like you to remember: Daisy. Knows. How. To. Spin."

Rachel smiled at my emphasis, then nodded.

"What is most important to remember?" I asked.

"That Daisy. Knows. How. To. Spin." Rachel imitated me so well we broke out in laughter.

Then I said, "We aren't going to spin. I'd like you and Daisy to take a little walk, and right there by that poop pile she so graciously left us, I'd like you to turn and go the other way. But you're going the other way because you just got a text alert on your phone."

Rachel smiled and said, "So you want me to—"

I raised my hand and said, "I'd like you *and* Daisy to walk to that poop pile, etcetera, etcetera." I made the observation that when she talked to me about loping Daisy, she had used the language of togetherness. When she talked about the spin, or even thought of doing it, it was just Daisy.

"Let's change that way of thinking a little bit. Both of you know how to do this."

Rachel walked Daisy off, and at the manure pile, they pivoted to their right with ease before continuing to walk toward me.

"That's your spin," I smiled.

"Well, technically…"

I laughed and said, "Let's drop the technical aspect for now, shall we?" Rachel humored me and rode to the manure pile again, this time pivoting left and walking back toward me.

"Okay," she sighed. "You're right. It's easy. Which means it was me who was messing Daisy up."

"Rachel, in her world, you don't mess anything up. She thought you wanted her to go slowly, or maybe she thought she was doing something wrong, so she went slowly because she wasn't confident about what you were asking. This has very little to do with your skill as a rider and more to do with a miscommunication."

She sighed and nodded.

After doing the exercise a couple more times, we changed it.

"Starting to feel more like loping, isn't it?"

Rachel nodded, relaxing into the smile that was bigger than when we started.

"Now, when you go toward the poop pile, do the same thing, and then add a second pivot so you're going back in the direction you started. Like you just got that text, and then your mean instructor says, 'Get back here and ignore your phone!'"

Rachel and Daisy walked toward the pile, pivoted right and then pivoted right again before stopping.

"That's it!" I shouted. Though I've known since I was a little girl that horses don't appreciate sudden, loud noises, in this instance, I couldn't help celebrating what they had just done: a relaxed spin that had relaxed movement behind it.

Rachel beamed before saying, "That's all?"

"Yes! That's all! Daisy knows this skill. All it takes is for us to get out of her way long enough so she can do it."

"I'd like to try a lope circle to a spin." I could tell Rachel was determined to conquer this frustration.

"Here's the deal: I'd like you to relax and offer the spin the same way you've been doing."

"Deal!" she said, almost before I'd finished speaking. She and Daisy moved off into a lope almost from a standstill, then spiraled into a spin right by the pile of manure. Rachel's hair was lifted by the same wind that lifted Daisy's spun-silk tail. Mystery solved.

151

It's not easy for us to have confidence in the idea that less is more, especially with horses. We're taught that if a horse isn't doing something, we need to add more stuff. I've found that by doing less and slowing down, we can get further, faster, than speeding it all up. Plus, being buried in cues can't be fun.

Cues are like individual conversations. One cue is an intimate chat with a friend. Two cues, a group text. Three or more cues? A debate run amok.

Most of the time, it's not only the number of cues, but the type of cues we're using. A rein and a leg will provoke a different quality of movement than a breath and an intention. Breathing and holding an intention also lets us use fewer of whatever cues we need, because the horse is already listening at a certain level.

As Rachel brought Daisy back over to me, I said, "You'll need to make sure there's a pile of manure in the right spot at your shows."

Rachel laughed and said, "I cannot believe it was that simple."

"Well," I said. "Simple, but sometimes not easy."

THE HORSE INSIDE

I often hear myself saying, "Treat your horse as though he's your friend." This doesn't come up with every horse and rider. And it doesn't mean that people aren't already doing this to some degree; most of us have horses because we deeply care about and enjoy them. However, it's also the case that when our human hardwiring takes over, we can go from gentle and understanding to harsh and combative in the blink of an eye.

Once big emotions arise, it can be very difficult to keep a level head and a soft touch. Overthinking and being caught up in the world between our ears also creates barriers, so much so that, even if the horse does his best to connect with us, we can't hear or feel it.

This may be why (thankfully) so many other modalities are being applied to horses these days— from martial arts to Tai Chi, yoga, Neuro-Linguistic Programming, breathing techniques, energy work, and various bodywork methods.

We recognize that things aren't as separate as they seem. What works for us can also be applied to, and work for, horses. We recognize that what we carry inside us finds its way through us and into our horses. We recognize that breathing a little more slowly has positive effects on both ourselves and our horse. We understand that a relaxed body is a more supple body, and with that, our internal and external balance improves. We come to understand that if we practice how to *be* in our non-horse life, when we're with them, things get easier. Things feel better. There's less pressure to achieve perfection and more enjoyment of the horse's being-ness.

So what does "treat your horse as your friend" mean?

It means to recognize that, just like us, horses are capable of feeling many things. I don't think it's anthropomorphizing to say that horses feel fear, anxiety, worry, and confusion. They bruise, they ache, they bleed, they get stiff, they shut themselves away when they're frightened but can't physically escape.

Like us, when they're listened to, treated with respect, and communicated with clearly and consistently, they relax. They can rely on us to provide information in a way they understand, and if they can't understand us, they can rely on us not to punish them for it.

The wonderful news is that most horses want to connect and be with us. Horses are born with harmony, accord, understanding, and rapport preinstalled, and will engage with us on those levels if we give them the chance.

What does that chance look like? It could be making our horse's physical comfort a priority. From hooves to teeth and everything in between, we want to offer them the best we've got. This includes environment, food, and companionship with other horses. It includes being as skilled and knowledgeable as possible in a given moment so we can be clear and consistent in our interactions with them. Can we spend time with them without an agenda? When we reach a point of anger, frustration, confusion, doubt, or hopelessness, can we either put the horse away and try again another time, or pause, breathe, and set that feeling aside so we can be in as neutral a place as possible?

There are reasons we become and remain friends with people. They are supportive, don't have an agenda, are kind in their interactions, and listen well. There are other reasons, too, but these are the things I strive to bring to my horse, and certainly to my family, friends, and clients.

Horses, on the other hand, cannot choose with whom they interact. They can, however, choose whom they open up to, give more than they have to, and trust.

"What if," as one woman said to me with exasperation "they

don't act like my friend?" My reply: "You're their friend, and that's what matters." Her statement and the feeling with which she said it have stayed with me. I've turned it over in my head and heart. In fact, that age-old question arises with me as well: How do we remain open in the face of something that scares us, or makes us mad, or (even worse) makes us look or feel foolish? One of the intentions I've found helpful to remember is that when it comes to horses, what they're doing is not personal.

I'll say that again: It isn't personal.

If your horse is doing things you don't like or you aren't looking for, she's tired, in pain, confused, or afraid. Everything a horse does is information and, I believe, an attempt to communicate with us. It's up to us whether we listen and respond or carry on and hope the horse "gets over it." As we would with a human friend who's lost or scared or confused, we offer the horse help. Support. Understanding.

These ways of consideration create doorways where there were walls. Although no horse is obligated to open themselves to you, to show all they have within them, to trust that their vulnerabilities and strengths have a safe place to rest with you, creating doorways leads to rooms we didn't know were there.

For me, this is where the good stuff is. When we know ourselves and make choices in a way that others—horses or humans—can rely on, doors open. An eye that was dull sparks. A breath that was held is released. What we call magic, relationship, and heart arises from the ashes of discord, fear, and tension. It's all there. Inside the horse, and inside you, too.

JUDGING, THINKING, FEELING

In college, I had a friend who'd grown up with horses. He was tall and lanky and rode any horse under any circumstance. Calm horse, nervous horse, bucking horse, rearing horse, show-ring lope or gallop on a trail: he was on that horse's back with a smile on his face. At that time in my life and with my limited horse experience, I thought this was a trait to be admired. I thought riding a horse who didn't want to be ridden made my friend A Great Rider.

He showed locally and statewide in the Western classes, but he was gunning for The Congress, the largest Quarter Horse show in the country. The equipment he bought, the lessons he paid for, the money he spent on horses who had the kind of breeding he wanted was geared toward reaching this goal.

That meant a lot of shows over several years. It also meant that the guy I once knew as easy-going and happy shifted into someone who was never satisfied and ran down his fellow show friends behind their backs. I noticed that he was harder on his horses, and heard him grumble that his horses needed to be "taught a lesson" because they didn't perform the way he wanted them to.

At the time, I was helping him with his horses and getting a lesson or two in exchange. Those lessons went from filled with laughter and fun to increasingly tense. I started to hear more about my lack of skills than how to improve them. During the summer I went with him to shows, I also heard about all the other riders' lack of skill. Before I knew it, I was joining him in the kind of conversation you hope no one you're talking about overhears.

After that summer, I stopped spending time with him, largely because I had a semester's worth of classes that required me to invest more time in my schoolwork. It was also both convenient and necessary for me to distance myself from him. The more time I spent away from my friend and his harsh pronouncements, the better I felt—mostly about myself. I was glad I didn't have to hear his low opinions of other riders and watch as he bullied his horses.

You'd think my proclivity to judge others would've stopped there. It didn't. It took me a long time to figure out that if you're happy in your own life, and in your own skin, you have much less need to mete out unkind words about someone else.

When I was a little, I remember liking things or not liking things for pretty straightforward reasons. I liked reading, but didn't like PE. I liked dogs and cats and horses and my friends, but not the mean-girl group in my class. I liked the snow, but not walking to school in it.

When does it change? Somewhere along the rutted road to adulthood, we start to have more complicated reasons for liking or not liking. Our preferences take on so much weight. We pronounce and lecture on why one thing is better than something else, then fight about those reasons—most of the time, in unreasonable ways.

What's so difficult about saying, "I like this, but I don't like that"? Are we afraid to reveal ourselves, and so come to rely on complex judgments that we use as shields?

When our horse does something we don't like, do we *have* to claim that he's "being naughty," is "stubborn," or "has ADD"?

We don't have to, but we do.

Everyone's happy when horses behave themselves, when they contain their innate power and play by our rules. Not so much when they act like horses—wary of shadows and sniffing the breeze, velvet nostrils expanded to learn things we're deaf and blind to.

In the case of horses being horses, I think our judgments are a way to cover up the fact that we don't know what's going on, and more to the point, not knowing makes us nervous.

So, what do we do?

Next question: Do we have to *do* anything?

Over time, I've really worked on switching from judgment to thinking more clearly when I teach or ride. It recently occurred to me that I could, with a little effort, take whatever it is I'm doing in the arena and apply it to my life.

But oh! Climate change! Politics! Covid-19! And why doesn't he pull up those saggy jeans and put on a belt!?

A mind that's busy judging is also a tense mind. A tense mind usually produces tension in the body, and neither of these tensions will yield relaxation in our horse, whether we're on the ground or on the horse's back.

To perhaps oversimplify, some emotions and attitudes produce tension or tightening, and thus, closure in our bodies, while others create the opposite: openness and ease. Whatever the origin is, I know that riding with a brain that is assessing, planning, and judging is a sure way to feel dissatisfied. We miss half of the experience of being with our horse when we ride with only our brains engaged.

Anytime our mind tightens, our body will follow. In fact, I often wonder what happens first: did our horse become momentarily unbalanced and *then* we felt the wobble and our brain jumped into the fray? The art of being with horses is the ability to maintain as much relaxation in ourselves as possible no matter what our horse is up to. Hence the popularity of breathing and weaving other body-awareness disciplines into horsemanship.

As those practices teach us more about mindfulness, body awareness, and the power of deep breathing, we can access those feelings when we are with our horses.

Over the past couple of decades, I've followed the work of Byron Katie (who has a very interesting process for dealing with judgments); practiced breathwork, meditation, Buddhism; improved my diet; explored the martial art of Aikido; and increased the amount of exercise I get. All of these have helped not only lower my overall feelings of anxiety, but have given me constructive ways to deal with the judgment voice that crops up in my head. As this voice has calmed down, I find I can hear horses at a level I couldn't before. Usually—not always, but generally—I feel centered and able to be a better instructor as well as live with myself and others with more ease.

Thinking is difficult. Facing our inner truth is rarely a picnic. Thinking is what brains are designed to do. Judging stands at the other end of the spectrum of thinking. As Carl Jung says, "Thinking is difficult. That's why people judge." As we get older, it's easier to dismiss the body as just the way we carry around our magnificent brain. During the course of a day, I find it far easier to clutch onto judgment like it's a jelly doughnut I've been offered in place of a salad: I know the salad is better for me but oh, is that doughnut a heavenly rush or what?

It's likely that our ability to judge, assess, or discern is an evolutionary gift that got us where we are today. Without the ability to remember life-threatening events and make snap judgments if they arise again, humans would have died out a long time ago. Aside from our highly evolved brains, we have nothing else to compete with. Strip us down to a pair of shorts and a tank top and we can't run very far or fast, can't keep warm or stay cool without help, can't defend ourselves with teeth, claws, or antlers.

What do we have? A magnificent, dense-with-dendrites, complexly folded brain. And what do we do with that brain? We judge, assess, question, plan, and process, among other things. Go to any horse show or clinic, and if you sit amongst a crowd of people, you'll likely hear murmurings and sighs and the certainty of voice that signals knowing more than the horse and rider in the arena.

Judgment, in and of itself, is not a bad thing. Using it as a defense against anything we find threatening is probably natural. But just because it's natural doesn't mean it's benevolent. Hurricanes are natural, too. It's when we use judgment to blind ourselves to other realities that it gets in the way. Saying "I don't know" is often a surprisingly good corrective for the fever dream of judgment. The further we can distance ourselves from negatively judging things, the closer we'll come to seeing things clearly.

One of the thousands of reasons so many of us find being around animals restful is because they don't judge us. They accept us as we are in any given moment. Being around horses, especially horses who are in a calm and restful state, can bring us to their level. If we allow our brains to slow down along with our heart rate, we can begin to inhabit a place of relaxed alert-ness that is so effective when working with our horse.

I've come to realize that we are evolving from our heads into our bodies. From thinking into including how the world around us feels. From there, it's a natural step into our hearts. From brains to bodies to feelings, I believe we are growing in a way that lets us understand horses and ourselves without the thick veil of judgement. That particular veil can cloud a rich and nourishing experience. Connecting this triune centers us. Judgment quiets down, and peace finds us more often.

ONE REIN THOUGHTS

By the time Shelby came into the arena for her lesson, her mare's sorrel coat was almost black with sweat. When Shelby bought Jewel the previous year, she didn't see anything alarming about her behavior other than that the horse seemed a little more nervous than other horses she'd come across. But over the course of her first year with Shelby, Jewel had gone from nervous to an unpredictable runaway. Shelby, an older and experienced horsewoman, had zero desire to come off a horse at a full gallop, which is where I came in.

While she and I talked, I ran my hands under the Western saddle Jewel was wearing, checking the blanket and fit. I checked the bridle and made sure the bit was the right diameter. Shelby had gone to great lengths to customize everything for Jewel. She'd had the vet out to check her over, taken care of her teeth and feet, and made sure Jewel received bodywork every month.

The support Shelby had given Jewel was thorough and had, in some respects, helped. Jewel was quieter on the ground, she had gained some needed weight and muscle mass, and her runaway episodes had become infrequent. But she still began to sweat and move when Shelby saddled her, and usually had to canter in a round pen for fifteen to twenty minutes before Shelby would get on her. Shelby felt more confident in the sandy arena, knowing that even though Jewel ran, she wasn't uncontrollable.

As Shelby found the mounting block and got on Jewel, I saw the mare tense her whole body and then try to shoot forward. Before Jewel could rush more than a couple of strides, Shelby had bent the mare's head around to the stirrup and they circled in the middle of the arena.

That this was an established pattern became clear by the way Jewel quickly gave up and braced to a stop. Shelby held the mare in this position for a few seconds before releasing her and walking over to where I stood.

"So, is that normal?" I asked.

"Yes," Shelby said. "It doesn't happen every time, but it does happen enough that I'm ready for her."

I asked if Jewel had always felt the need to rush away when a rider was on her, and she said yes, but after learning the one-rein stop at another clinic she'd attended, at least she and Jewel weren't going too far.

"When you got her, she did this? Would she take off the moment a rider was on her?"

Shelby nodded. "I've had to use the one-rein stop more often in the last six months because if we go from walk to trot to canter, she goes faster than I'm asking. I'm not sure how to make her stop other than using one rein."

I asked them to walk down to the other end of the arena. As they turned, Jewel tightened up again but maintained a stiff walk. Shelby asked, "Do you want to see me trot her?" I watched as Jewel took two steps into her trot and then jumped into a lope that was more like a deer leaping in fright. Shelby grabbed one rein and pulled Jewel's head around, but this time, it took several minutes for the mare to come to a halt.

Walking up to the pair of them, I could see the whites of Jewel's eyes, and that her mouth was clamped shut. I suspected there was a miscommunication between her and Shelby, and mentioned that if we tried something different, maybe we could get both of them speaking the same language.

"Oftentimes, the one-rein stop is taught and used as a tool that's supposed to solve the problem of a horse who's going too fast. Sometimes, it's used as a punishment, because it's an effective way to control movement. But the downside is that a one-rein stop, if used often enough, can sometimes make a horse nervous about moving at all."

Shelby asked why it was taught so much, and why other trainers swore by it. I could tell she was confused, and concerned that she may have been inadvertently adding to Jewel's nervousness.

"Honestly? I don't know why other trainers use it so much. When I first started training, I used it a lot, too. It's an emergency brake of sorts, and it gives the rider a way to slow down a horse who's unable to respond to any sort of pressure.

"But here's the thing: it's quite often used as a band-aid. Meaning, a one-rein stop is a poor substitute for taking time to educate the horse about what stopping is. While it's good in an emergency, it's not very good as an everyday training strategy."

Then I explained how we were going to change what she was doing to help Jewel. Instead of pulling her head around to the stirrup, she would ask for a figure eight, a relatively small one that prevented Jewel from being in a straight line from nose to tail.

"What we want to do with Jewel is to give her a chance to release her energy instead of bottling it up. A one-rein stop is like boiling water in a kettle without a spout; it may work for a little bit but at some point, it's going explode from too much unreleased pressure."

I could see Shelby starting to put the pieces together, so I continued.

"I'm not saying never use the one-rein stop. What I am saying is that there are other, more effective ways to help your horse. I personally haven't used a one-rein stop in more than twenty years."

As Shelby asked Jewel to walk again, I talked about thinking of the shape of her figure eight and let her know her timing was good—that she could catch Jewel before she got too far into speeding up.

"Once you ask for the trot, let's put her in a little figure eight and see what happens," I said.

As Shelby asked for the trot and Jewel responded by a stiff leap into it, Shelby picked up her left rein and began riding Jewel into the figure eight. It was five minutes before Jewel could slow to a walk, but in that time, she had started to move with her head lower, and her body relaxed.

"Tell me again why that works," Shelby asked as she walked Jewel over to me.

"Well, it works not only because you've installed a spout on the kettle to let off the steam, but also because instead of saying to Jewel 'Don't do that!' You're giving her something positive to do. Think of it this way: All she knows is that when she goes faster, she ends up bent around and stopped. She doesn't know why, so this increases her anxiety, which increases her need to speed up.

"Her question to you has been, 'Can I speed up now?' The answer she's been getting doesn't make sense to her, so she keeps repeating the question. By directing her into a figure eight, you're not only giving her a way to release nervousness and energy, you're saying 'Yes, and if you need to go fast, we'll go in a figure eight.'"

As Shelby and Jewel kept practicing, I could see the tightness melt from both of their bodies. Jewel was able to move into a trot without rushing and Shelby started to feel more confident about how she was answering Jewel's question. By the end of our session, Shelby could ask Jewel for a trot and she would jog and then come back down with minimal rein pressure.

With horses, when an unwanted behavior shows up, we often ask the wrong question: "How can I fix it?" A more useful question might be, "Why is my horse doing this in the first place?" The first question will most often put us behind the horse, not only in timing but in finding an effective solution. The second will lead us to explore our interactions and come up with ways to help and educate our horse. An educated horse is most often a calmer and more content horse.

MASTERS OF PATTERNS

As humans, we distinguish between planning to do something and actually doing it. I've also noticed that we spend a whole lot of time on the former and sometimes zero on the latter.

Horses don't make that distinction. Like Yoda, they either do something or they do not. So when we're riding, if we're kinda, sorta thinking about perhaps sometime, maybe someday, trotting, and our horse trots? Technically, the horse got the correct answer. We can celebrate how smart, willing, and tuned-in they are.

But what more often happens is that we get frustrated, pull on the reins, and holler "My horse is anticipating me!"

As if this is a bad thing.

Humans ascribe far more to horses than horses are physiologically hardwired to give. The very word "anticipating" implies two elements: the ability to accurately predict the future and the ability to analyze a situation and draw conclusions from it. Both of these functions take place in the neocortex, which is quite large in the human brain but rather small in the horse brain. For humans, the neocortex analyzes, plans, and plays a role in complex emotions and behavior inhibition, for example, wanting to do something, then realizing it's not socially or morally appropriate and refraining from doing it. What we know about the cortex in horses is that it is used largely for voluntary movements.

All living things—humans and horses included—seek comfort and avoid pain. A barn or paddock; herd mates; the sights, smells, and sounds of familiar surroundings. All of these contribute to a sense of familiarity that brings the horse comfort and peace of mind. Anyone who's spent time around animals (not just horses) has witnessed them seeking this comfort. Humans are similar in this regard.

A known task or skill—for example, side passing—will give the horse less worry simply because it's familiar. When a particular cue is given by the rider, the horse knows to move sideways. Now, if we take that same horse and ask him to learn an unfamiliar skill—say, a flying lead change—his anxiety level will naturally rise. Different horses will experience different levels of that rise depending upon how they were taught in the past, what kind of relationship they have with their rider, or if they've been hurried or physically forced into learning. If the worry is great enough, the horse will go back to a skill or behavior for which he is sure of the outcome. Or, sometimes, he will rush through what he thinks you want. In either case, the horse is about as far away from "anticipating" something as we are from sprouting a mane and tail.

Most of the time, horses will behave in one of two ways: from instinct or from a learned response. Horses will also rely on trust in a relationship they have with a person. The instinct is theirs, the learned response comes from their environs or, much of the time, from humans. The next time you're with your horse and you find the phrase, "My horse is anticipating me," running through your head, pause for a moment, step out of a very human thought, and see if you can pinpoint whether he's trying to tell you something else. The simple act of listening often brings surprising results.

I like to think of it as the Wizard of Oz in reverse: What's behind the curtain is so much bigger and brighter than what we see in front of the curtain. What's behind the veil of our sensory perceptions holds a vast amount of insight. If we part the curtains of our senses just a little bit, we can often glean information that would otherwise not have registered had we only paid attention to the puppet show our senses put on for us.

Really, what is happening is twofold: We have knowingly or unknowingly repeated a pattern and the horse is following it. Or, we spent so much time planning before asking that the horse just went ahead and did it. As I see it, this is great. Wonderful, even. We have chosen to get to know a creature who, by some miracle, not only appears to be overwhelmingly talented at reading us but is also willing to go along with our plans.

Think about it. If you knew what a co-worker or friend wanted to do—if it was clear as day and was being telegraphed every second and you heard and felt it—would you want to go along with their every plan?

Horses do this all the time.

Horses are also masters of patterns. If you show them something the same way often enough, they will start to rely on and trust the pattern. It's part of their evolutionary makeup; knowing the route to water or where to find food or a shady spot on a blisteringly hot day was how they survived. It's how they still survive, even though their roaming area is usually much smaller than their ancestors'. Add that they now have room service (i.e., humans), and you can see how little time it takes them to figure out the cues that means it's feeding time.

Many years ago, a horse's roaming area was vast. Humans weren't around when horses were about the size of a Great Dane, but my guess is that many of the things that happen now also happened then. Rivers may dry up, but given enough rain, they will flow in roughly the same area. Grassy plains stretch for hundreds of miles and though subject to wildfire or drought, they were rarely affected across their entire extent. If there were big changes, the horses did what horses do best. They moved until they found somewhere more hospitable.

Once we brought horses into our lives, they lost the freedom to seek out different environments. We are their environment; we are the food-providers, we decide the how and what and why and when of every day for them.

We may be experts at thinking, and it may have brought us far, but horses are masters of moving, sensing, and responding to ensure they stay alive.

All of this is to say that there's a mountain of untapped potential right outside in your paddock.

The next time you're with your horse, do a little experiment. Think less. Feel and do more. Trust your good intentions. Trust your horse to do his best to do what you are asking. Trust that you won't mess it up. But even if you do make a muck of things, it's okay. Because besides being great at connecting, horses are also good at overlooking our shortcomings.

We can work with their skills and knowledge or try to change or fight them. Either way, the horse will go on being a horse; they will find comfort in their life or they won't. Interacting with horses isn't always easy, and we don't always get it right. I do believe, though, that if we make it a priority to act more and think less, we can get further and become closer to our horses than even we can anticipate.

PRACTICE MAKES PURPOSE

Long days of staying at home and learning to navigate a Covid-19 virus world had me feeling like crawling under a warm blanket until it was over. Every day during the initial two-month lockdown, my husband and I were in one of three places: at home, at the grocery store going the wrong way down the one-way aisles, or at the barn, taking care of the horses.

The barn is where my sanity is. On days when all I feel is troubled, for a few hours I have a purpose. Cleaning stalls, filling water troughs and buckets, putting out feed, making mashes for our older horses.

It's probably one of my favorite purposes of all. Some days, I'll take a couple of brushes out to the paddock and brush each horse. Early spring is the itchiest time of year for them, so no halter is needed to keep them in place. They practically line up when they see it's Grooming Day.

When staying in bed with a book holds far more attraction than getting up, it's the call of our horses and their need for equine services that motivates me to pull on my jeans, put on my hat, and eat something so I don't pass out while forking manure into the wheelbarrow.

During this difficult time, I discovered how important purpose is to our well-being. Whether we're just trying to get through a day or figure out how to do a trot-to-canter transition with our horse, a sense of purpose goes a long way toward engaging both states of mind.

If we ask our horses to do something, and we kinda mean it,

or we're kinda distracted by the news we read just before riding, or we're kinda tired, or kinda hungry, our lack of purpose will translate for our horse as him kinda doing the task. Horses are the world's most beautiful mirrors.

Watching the clouds over the mountain on a particularly grim day, I reflected that there I was, standing in the sunshine, listening to the birds, gazing at a view people travel to Colorado from all over the world to see, focusing on how awful I felt. No one made me do this. I woke up feeling awful and indulged it. I chose it over beauty.

Well, if I choose to feel badly, I could also choose to feel better. So I did. I started by being grateful for all I saw, and for the warmth of the day. With every negative thought, with every spike of anxiety, I tried to find something I was grateful for.

It didn't make my dark mood evaporate, but at least I became aware of the sunlight. I became aware that despite our moods, having a purpose shifts our attitude. Whether that shift is tiny or huge, the potential is there.

When we bring a sense of purpose to our time with horses, even if it's to go for a nice walk, be together while we groom them, or listen more closely, we gain a fuller experience of what it means to be with and understand them.

One summer, I was getting Rocky ready for a hunter/jumper schooling show. Rocky has been mentally fit for years; my goal was to help his body be fit enough to jump one round of 2-foot, 6-inch jumps. Our friend and my jumping instructor, Dev Branham (who owns and trains at his hunter/jumper barn near Houston, Texas), was game to ride Rocky at a schooling show, and we thought it would be fun for Rocky to experience a full round of jumps. However, we made a vow that if at any time, Rocky showed physical or mental signs that preparing for a jumping show was hard on him, we would stop.

Everything we did together had purpose. I kept a close eye on how long it took Rocky to recover from jumping and adjusted his diet to help his body stay strong. We rode him as we always did, with softness and clarity, but the particular purpose—to take him to a show where he could jump a round—guided all our activities. We did three to four jumps twice a week; the rest of the time, it was flat work. I looked to Rocky to maintain my own sense of fun and joy about the process.

During those four months, I noticed that I couldn't give into my perfection posse: "We are going to a show, we have to be perfect!" While having the purpose of taking Rocky to a show tempted my old perfection habits to resurface, they were always replaced by something that sounded like Beethoven's *Ode To Joy*. What a wonderful opportunity to change how I felt about showing, and a great opportunity to show that posse right out the door. Symphony over cacophony, that was my new motto.

A month before the show, Colorado experienced an outbreak of an equine disease that was highly contagious. I watched as this disease made its way across the state, and finally into our area. Before I knew it, the jumping show had been cancelled and the barn we ran our summer clinics out of had a case and was quarantined.

Disappointment is sometimes too small a word for a big feeling. As I put away Rocky's new bridle and saddle pad, I wondered if we would ever have another chance to take him to a show. That was 2019, and he was twenty-one. I didn't know if we could ask him to do a round of jumps the next year when he would be twenty-two. It seemed that our purpose had been taken away.

When I woke up the morning after the show was cancelled, I realized that Rocky was fine. He knew his purpose in any given moment. I was the one agonizing over an opportunity that, to be honest, he hadn't any knowledge of or need to do. While I was grieving the loss of an experience—seeing him do something he loves with a skilled rider—he was munching hay and feeling perfectly content. This is what I love about horses, and all animals. Their presence in the *now* of life is so powerful that it can remind us to live there, too.

Luckily, purposes can change. That day, after talking with Dev, we decided we'd build our own course. So, on the last day of the last clinic of the summer of 2019, Dev jumped Rocky over eight 2-foot, 6-inch jumps. It was a great round, and Rocky grew more determined with each jump. By the last jump, his ears were laid back and he was staring with determination at the far side of the hurdle. I have a photo of that moment. There's the blue sky and Rocky, body stretched with effort over a jump he cleared by an extra six inches.

These days, it seems my purpose is to find and live in these moments of joy. A rich life isn't one in which we surround ourselves with things or generate stuff. For me, a rich life is watching a yellow bee on a purple thistle. Rain slanting in sheets across the Rocky Mountains. Sunshine on my bare skin. A horse, and a friend, defying gravity and racing time.

IT'S NOT A CATCHING
PROBLEM

Our new clinic horse, Top, is a chocolate bay with a kind eye and a pink spot on his lower lip that makes him look like his tongue is always out. He came to us from South Dakota, and before that, he was a working ranch horse. Top is ten years old. Undoubtedly, he knows stuff.

We usually buy ranch horses because they tend to be quiet. They don't mind standing tied and are easy to haul. They're easy to get around. Since we need them to do the specific job of being a clinic horse, "easy to get around" is important.

The first two months we had Top, he would turn his hindquarters to us and trot away when we walked into the pen. It took an average of two to three minutes to talk him into being caught. At one point, Mark did a few minutes of asking Top to bring his head toward him (instead of his hindquarters), but other than that, we hadn't had a chance to work on Top's feeling better about this particular skill.

Top, like most of the ranch horses we've bought, has a hard time with being caught. Once we're close to him with a halter, it's usually not a big deal. But that first five minutes or so, he feels he needs to run, or duck behind another horse, or look for a way out that he might've missed earlier.

Over the years, I've come to understand that this kind of behavior is not about being caught. It's not a catching problem, nor is it really any kind of problem at all. The horse's stress level has gone up. Moving is how they find their way out of being stressed or confused.

Horses who are in some sort of discomfort, whether from their feet, their teeth, or their body, are more reluctant to be caught. Some horses who have a hard time doing the job assigned to them will also take a while to allow themselves to be caught. Maybe they don't understand their role; maybe their job causes them stress or worry or fear. Maybe the person handling them is rougher than the horse is comfortable with. Maybe grooming is uncomfortable, or the horse has ulcers, or the saddle doesn't fit or is being girthed up too quickly.

Catching, like most things relating to horses, is one piece of a larger puzzle. And, as most humans do, when we're trying to decipher the whole, we tend to focus on one small piece. We stare at it with uneasy intensity, thinking that if we could get more light, or stronger glasses, or a frame for it, we could tell what the whole picture is.

Put all of these puzzle pieces together, and now we see the fuller picture. The horse who's "hard to catch" is actually trying to tell us something.

We often need to help a horse learn how we'd like the catching process to go. For us, it's by stopping and facing us instead of turning away and running, but there are lots of other ways as well. We focus on keeping the stress level as low as we can and building on good behavior instead of punishing the behavior we don't want.

As for Top, I've never thought he was particularly difficult to catch, and neither did Mark. We look at all horse behavior as communication. At any given moment, horses are doing their best to let us know how they're feeling. How they feel and how they act are the same states of being for them. The fact that Top needed to move away from us told us more about how he felt than anything else. He wasn't being "naughty," he wasn't being "stubborn." The only thing he was being was worried.

So what changed that picture for Top? We had his teeth

balanced, and we had a chiropractor work on him. A month later, I gave him a Masterson Method® bodywork session. He has a saddle that fits, his feet were already in good shape, and the saddle pads we use are memory foam–based. When we go out to halter him, the halter goes on with consideration for being in such close proximity to his face. In other words, gently.

From the time we halter him to the time we turn him out at the end of our workday, we handle him as softly as possible. We do our best to be clear with him.

When we were giving clinics in North Carolina, we put Top and Rocky out in a large paddock that had a shelter. In the morning when we went out to get them, Top drifted away from us at a walk, then turned and faced us. I didn't feel an elevation in his concern or energy level; his head was low and his walk was swingy. Walking away from a person with a halter is now just a habit that he doesn't need. Like all habits, it will take some time to be replaced with a new one.

When Top walked away, neither Mark nor I changed our pace or our breathing. We didn't spin the lead ropes and "make him leave faster." Top drifted to our right, so we changed direction to the right and walked parallel to him before he stopped and turned, ears forward, and body relaxed.

Saying a horse has a "catching problem" is really a way of giving ourselves permission to stare at one tiny piece of the whole puzzle of that horse, instead of finding the other pieces so we can see what the whole picture actually may be.

It's a little intimidating to think that we might be doing something our horse isn't comfortable with, and change is sometimes pretty danged difficult. It's far easier to slap a label on the behavior and let the label do the talking.

It's sometimes danged difficult for horses, too, but we ask them to change all the time. Seems to me that fair's fair—we can do some changing right along with them.

BREE RETURNS

I didn't know I needed to see Bree until I saw her again. Five years had passed since she and I had the accident that put me in the hospital with a small brain bleed. For five years, she had been fostered by a kind Texas horsewoman who took her in as a companion for another Arabian. But life is filled with switchbacks and steep hills, and the woman's life changed. When she texted us that she needed to find Bree a new home, we decided to take back my mare.

As we traveled from North Carolina to Texas, panic stole my breath when I thought about seeing Bree again. When we arrived at Bree's foster home, I watched from inside the truck as she was led to the trailer, and noticed it rock when Mark loaded her in. I felt my heart rate rise and found myself sweating so much that my t-shirt stuck to my back. I don't remember much of the half-hour drive back to the clinic venue, but I do remember breathing deeply and letting the wind from the open window dry me off. Once we were at the venue, Mark unloaded Bree and put her in the paddock with our two geldings. I watched her from outside the pen, then—feeling a recurrence of the earlier hyperventilating coming on—turned away and sat down in the shade.

Knowing a little about trauma and its aftereffects, this level of panic didn't surprise me. The intensity did, however. As I watched Bree look for grass in the Texas paddock, I realized that I felt the same as I had five years earlier, when I'd watched her through the fog of painkillers I was sent home from the hospital with. Fear was doing its best to convince me that time hadn't passed, and that I really didn't have the tools to deal with this. "There's a monster in the paddock!" my fear shouted that day.

The next day was humid and windless, and as I walked by the horse pen, I broke out into a sweat again, but this time, because the air was as thick as the water I'd just drunk. I called Bree's name ("Ree-ah!") using the tone I'd adopted when we were together. Her head popped up, her ears came forward, and she walked up to the fence, standing close to me and breathing quietly, reaching out to touch my face and shoulder with her nose. As instant as the fear had come, it was replaced with a joy that washed through me. This is why I'd loved her; the gratitude I was feeling was far bigger than my fear.

For the next three days, I took care of her while we worked. When I called her name, she came to me. We shared quiet moments, with her sniffing my belly and arms and shoulders and me stroking her silky neck. It felt natural to halter her. It was easy to groom her and put on her fly mask. I led her between paddocks and her stall and wasn't afraid, even when she snorted, flung her dainty head, and pranced. Sometimes, wildness needs to be celebrated, after all.

The only thing I felt was admiration for her beauty. The familiarity and ease that I experienced when I handled her was a safe place for both of us. It wasn't just that I've led a lot of horses. It was that I was leading Bree, and we'd written years of our own personal history. Both of us had now opened a new chapter in the book we shared. It was my fear that turned the accident into a 900-pound monster.

Bree helped me see that there were no monsters in the paddock.

We got back to Colorado just days before the quarantine went into effect, and on the way home, dropped Bree off at Happy Dog Ranch, where our friends had kindly arranged a place for her. Here, she could be a lesson horse for groundwork sessions, a safe horse for beginners to groom and learn with, and an addition to their therapy program. This life suited her far better than the one I could give her, one in which she would have minimal interaction with people because of our work schedule.

Before we left the next morning, we moved Bree from the paddock with our two geldings and put her in a round pen close to the herd. She was upset at first, running and calling to her friends. I knew how she felt; my mare had returned and now I was leaving her, albeit in a home where I knew her intelligence, gentleness, and grace would be appreciated. I was tempted to go into the round pen and run and holler myself.

Instead, I watched how her long, black tail flagged in the wind. How with each stride, she seemed unfettered by gravity. How she snorted, came to a walk, and grabbed mouthfuls of hay and sips of water.

I knew she would calm down and come to feel safe in her new life. I knew my friends at Happy Dog Ranch would value and love her, and that she would help many people feel better. I also knew that I would be able to see her more often and share those quiet moments that hadn't disappeared, despite our long separation.

It's funny how some relationships grow, disappear, and stay gone, and others continue to grow in spite of distance and time. After our accident, I knew that by placing Bree in a foster home, I was doing the best I could for her at that moment, and made peace with my decision to have her live elsewhere.

Then when she returned, and after my terror faded, I realized that she and I had both grown in our own ways. When we had a chance to spend time together again, it was as though no time at all had passed. She was the same sweet, beautiful mare I had loved, and that love hadn't gone anywhere. Rather, it had, like our hearts, expanded.

This is the gift of a good horse: without design or artifice, manipulation or grand plans, they bring us to the realization of how to be a good human, and in so doing, to grow beyond what we thought was possible. Sometimes, what we consider to be a 900-pound monster is really a 900-pound gift waiting for us to open it.

THE SEASON OF CHANGE

There are things I like about the end of the year and its holidays. The lights that wrap around the trees on our downtown's main street are beacons, especially after a nighttime snowfall. I like being reminded by the dark to go inside and recharge after a season of working from light's beginning to light's end. I like the kindness I see being given and received more often than at other times of the year. It's a good reminder that kindness is a good gift, no matter what the season is. I also like spending time with family, and, despite my allergy to cooking, I even like planning meals that we share around a big table with people we love.

When I think about why I sometimes feel so stressed despite the "joy of the season," it really comes down to one thing: the impending doom of Christmas day.

Being plugged into the internet is just not a good idea this time of year. From late October onward, it's a commercial scrum: Who can have more sales? Who can score the biggest Black Friday win? But wait! Now there's cyber Monday!

It's not like December 25 is a surprise either; live through enough Christmases and you know what to expect; you have a general idea what your friends and family members would enjoy receiving; and you know that by that date, everything will come together (or not).

Every year, I felt myself winding up like a too-tight rope around a thick saddle horn: December 25 is the cow horse, and I am the steer. Every year, I had the same emotional response

I did the year before it: race to get everything done on top of everything that already needs to be done until I am snappy and tired and sick of my own self.

Last year, it occurred to me that instead of fighting the march of time across the calendar, I could take a more active role and begin sorting out Christmas in October. If I got really proactive, maybe June! I could waltz through a holiday season with less stress, more rest, and as a more pleasant person. I could accept that time, and the calendar, pause for no one.

We're capable of sorting these kinds of things out for ourselves. But what happens when we start seeing the first signs that a beloved horse may need a change too? That's what happened with Rocky, one of our own beloved horses.

January 2010

Mark and I walk out on the thirty-five-acre pasture where the horses winter, and I call "Hooo-rses!" Six furry heads pop up from eating and they gallop toward us, coming to a walk several yards away before greeting us with a whuff of warm breath that mists the cold morning air.

It's the beginning of our clinic season, which means that Rocky and two other horses will be joining us as we work around the country.

We halter Rocky and the other geldings and hold them for the vet so he can write up health certificates. After he's done, we turn the horses loose once more. Two of the geldings walk away, noses lowered in a search for the grass under the snow. Rocky stays, and we give him a pat on the neck before walking to the truck. He follows us back to the gate, hangs his head over the green rails, and watches us walk away.

He's always been like this; eager to work, greeting us first, easy to catch.

December 2019

Rocky has traveled over a million miles in a horse trailer. He's stood quietly in hot and cold weather, rainstorms and wild winds, city traffic, and along desert highways. That's a lot of time for his hooves to be disconnected from the earth. He's twenty-one and has been doing his job with excellence since he was seven. He's earned his "Rock Star" nickname.

He's stood calmly while other horses worried. He's helped our less-experienced clinic horses get to know the job. He's a ranch horse, a trail horse, a clinic horse; has worked cattle, starred in a movie, and given a rides to folks who want to feel how soft true softness is. During the last four years, he's been teaching me how to jump.

In the last year, though, we noticed some quiet changes. Instead meeting us at the gate, Rocky often waited for us to come to him to put on his halter. He's harder to keep weight on when we travel, and he no longer finishes the hay we hang in front of him during long hauls.

Last summer, while Mark was riding him, he refused three times to get close to a horse Mark was trying to help through a gate. When Mark asked Rocky to step in a little closer, Rocky didn't move.

Instead of using a stronger cue, Mark let it go and finished the workday. He later admitted that Rocky's time as a clinic horse was done. Our red horse, who had never said no to anything we'd asked of him, refused three times in the space of as many minutes.

He was the first to go out on pasture that winter.

Now, as we walk over the grass pushing through the snow, I call to them "Hoooor-ses!" Up pop four furry heads, and they gallop toward us, Rocky leading the way.

This day, we need to trim their feet. All four horses stand

quietly in the winter sun as we chat with our farrier. Rocky goes first, and after he's done, we turn him loose. With barely a backward glance, he gallops away without waiting for the other horses, or for us. As we drive away, I look back at the green pipe gate and see only the winter field.

At some point, all of us will have to let our good old horses rest. We will have to read their signs and listen closely when they begin telling us they can no longer do what they used to. This is, of course, what we do for Rocky. He doesn't owe us a thing; it is we who owe him. Acceptance is simple if we look at how well our horses navigate it. It is just what it exactly is, no more, no less.

For me, however, this new chapter is a braid of emotions: one strand for sadness, one strand for gratitude, and one strand for curiosity.

I'm sad that Rocky has reached his age so quickly. I'm grateful we've had the pleasure of his company and his big, kind, generous heart. I'm curious because I'd like to find out where his yeses still are.

Now, any activities we in which we include Rocky are done with care and limits. We recognize that his spirit will probably always gallop ahead of his body. We accept that it's time for our good red horse to keep his hooves connected to the earth and go a little easier in this world.

AFTERWORD

Thorny, an old cowboy my parents knew, introduced me to horses when I was about three years old. In a faded photo recording that momentous event, I'm holding on to the lead rope of a gray speckled pony who wasn't a whole lot taller than I was.

Thorny was an old cowboy, rancher, and horse trader. He's the first person who looked me in the eye and asked me how much I thought the horse he was working with weighed. When I guessed 975 pounds, his craggy face broke into a smile as he told my parents they had a "real horse gal" on their hands.

Thorny seemed like he had a million horses. On another visit, my parents remember putting me up on a big red horse, where I sat smiling and clutching his copper mane until they lifted me down. That's when the screaming started. Other kids cried when they were lifted up on the horse's back. I cried when I was lifted off.

It was a portent of things to come. That day with the pony, I met magic; it was my version of getting an admission letter to Hogwarts. Like many "horse-crazy" kids, I pretended my bike was a horse, and sometimes ran around our backyard neighing. Collected Breyer models and made up pedigrees and voices for them. Fed grass to horses through fences and tried not to get caught. Really, who could have designed a more perfect animal? They smell good when they sweat; they smell good when they breathe; and when their hooves strike the earth in three-time, it's an invitation to unadulterated bliss. They're fuzzy and soft, and when they look at you with those eyes! When their ears flick back to catch your voice! A nicker makes my heart burst.

As an adult, I'm living with and teaching about the mystery that is the horse. While I still enjoy riding, I've discovered that the gifts horses offer us go beyond sitting on their backs. In my own evolution with horses, many things have captured my interest, and many horses have given themselves so that I might, for a little while, enter their world. So that I might, for a moment, feel the twin freedom of speeding across the ground while being free from the weight of it.

I'm no longer a little girl. I recently hit a milestone birthday, and though I've not usually been one to count years or label myself by them, I've also become increasingly aware of how challenging it is to age. Our bodies change, grief finds us more frequently, we listen as our doctor tells us about the invasive health screenings we must endure. Health insurance goes up and energy goes down.

But along with all of that, I also notice the frost on a horse's whiskers in the winter. How, on a chilly morning, the wind catches the mist of their breath. How standing beside them allows me to calm down and experience a grounded sense of peace. The rhythmic sound of horses chewing. Watching them gather hay into their mouths. Feeling their warm whuffing breath on my hands or face is the best self-care of all.

For me, horses are sacred.

In their veins, whether pureblood or born of unknown dam and sire, the horse carries the memories of battles and races, kindness and cruelty, nobility and work.

Throughout history, horses have been revered as members of a family, have been used on hard cobblestone streets pulling a cart, farmed expanses of open land, raced the wind and each other to claim titles that matter no more to them than the fly that alights on their gravity-defying legs. They've built regimes and countries and changed shapes and sizes hundreds of times throughout their history.

When my own love of all things horse went beyond a mere phase and turned into a way of life, I had the opportunity to step from a horse world that spoke using words of domination to a different world, one where words such as *partnership*, *communication*, and *relationship* are used.

All the times I've struggled, all the horrible things I've said to myself about my horsemanship; all the questioning, agonizing, and striving; bringing horses into my life and letting them go again—all of it! Yet, still, I can stand beside a horse and become mesmerized when the light shines through a rumpled mane. Horses are deep oceans encased in soft coats. Whether I'm riding or not, the feeling of being in a freefall around a horse is still mystical.

It all started with a dappled pony. Inside somewhere is that girl who still sneaks grass to horses through fences. Though I don't know how or when my horse journey will end, I do know I will always love and be grateful for horses.

ACKNOWLEDGMENTS

I wouldn't be the horse person I am today without the help of my husband Mark. His quiet ways and deep compassion for horses have inspired me for two decades. His kindness as a person and support as my partner through life are two steady rocks I lean on.

Thank you to my mom, Susan Tasaki, for editing this book and helping it become better. Her excellence as an editor is only surpassed by her brilliance at being a mom.

To my family, Dan, Erika, Keyvnn, and Quinn. I love you all more than I can express.

To Anna Blake, who provided the perfect subtitle for this book. Friendship is a beautiful gift, and one I am grateful to share with her.

And big thanks to you as well, for reading this book, for being on a journey with your horse, and for seeking out ways to live with horses that are based in kindness and understanding. The more we understand horses, the more we are able to improve their lives.

Made in the USA
Columbia, SC
04 January 2021

30311908R00121